Church
Advertising

Church
Advertising
A Practical Guide

Steve Dunkin

Creative Leadership Series
Lyle E. Schaller, Editor

Abingdon / Nashville

CHURCH ADVERTISING: A PRACTICAL GUIDE

Copyright © 1982 by Abingdon

Library of Congress Cataloging in Publication Data

DUNKIN, STEVE, 1949–
  Church advertising, a practical guide.
  (Creative leadership series)
  Includes bibliographical references.
  1. Advertising—Churches.   2. Church publicity.
  I. Title.   II. Series.
  BV653.D85   254.4   81-17562   AACR2

ISBN 0-687-08140-8

MANUFACTURED BY THE PARTHENON PRESS AT
NASHVILLE, TENNESSEE, UNITED STATES OF AMERICA

To
my wife Diane
and
all my faithful supporters at
Chippawa Presbyterian Church,
who together
made this book possible

Foreword

What does a young minister do when called to serve a hundred-fifty-year-old numerically declining church? How does that new pastor respond to the expectations of those members who want that decline reversed? What action steps might that new minister take?

Responses to those questions constitute the overall theme of this volume. In part, this is the story of what Steve Dunkin did when he came to a demoralized congregation that had built a new educational wing for what had appeared at the time to be a growing Sunday school, which later experienced a 70 percent decline in enrollment.

A second theme of this book can be stated in the question, What should the recently arrived minister do during the first year or two of a new pastorate? Take plenty of time to get to know everyone and build the trust level? That is a widely advocated piece of conventional wisdom. Or should the new minister assume the role of the enabler, equipping the saints to go forth and do ministry and thus enabling *them* to reverse the numerical decline and renew the psychological climate? Or should the minister recognize that it is impossible to "out passive" the passive members of a declining congregation? Should that pastor decline the mantle of leadership offered by the people when they go out looking for a new leader? The discussion of the role of the initiating leader alone makes this book worth the time of every minister who is contemplating a move to a new pastorate.

A third theme of this volume, and perhaps the point at which the author makes his most distinctive contribution, is the concept of stimulating numerical growth through the use of advertising.

While this may be difficult for some readers to believe, there are congregations in North America in which it is difficult to find members willing to go out and do visitation evangelism! That is the best single approach to church growth. For churches that find it difficult to enlist members for that purpose, however, the second-best approach is *effective advertising.* This also is a productive complementary strategy for congregations that *are* able to recruit callers for other approaches.

In this volume Steve Dunkin introduces the readers to the basic principles of advertising, and he follows this with detailed step-by-step procedures that will enable any congregation to develop its own strategy.

For some congregations the local newspaper may be the most effective vehicle for advertising. There is a detailed chapter on that subject which, among other points, explains the difference between strategies for reaching church-going readership and those for reaching the unchurched. In other communities, direct mail advertising may be the most productive channel, and advice on this is given in chapter 7. Radio, along with signs, billboards, and other media are discussed in later chapters. There are at least six hundred Christian radio stations on the North American continent, and this is often a very cost-effective method.

Finally, the author responds to the questions, What if it works? What if strangers begin to come to our church? What can we do to accommodate them—to make them feel welcome?

This is not a book for passive church leaders who believe salvation is to be found in reducing the size of the church budget. This is a book for creative and venturesome leaders who are seeking new channels for reaching people with the good news of Jesus Christ, who are open to new ideas, who are willing to take risks, and who can build on the experience of others. For those creative leaders, this volume can open new doors, enabling them to expand the evangelistic outreach of their churches.

Lyle E. Schaller
Yokefellow Institute
Richmond, Indiana

Contents

I

"In the Beginning . . ."

"My name is Dorwin Smith," the dapper older gentleman said as he extended his hand, "and this is my wife, Marjorie. And I'd like you to meet Winn and Phyllis Cornell. We've come from Chippawa Presbyterian Church in Niagara Falls, and we would like to talk with you."

It was early September, and we were standing just outside the front door of the small rural church where I had been serving since my ordination two years earlier. I had been hoping for a call to another church for a number of months, but so far had received nothing but refusals in response to my inquiries. Then suddenly the evening before, I had received a call from a vacant church in a small city not far away, intimating that some of the committee members would be in our church the next morning. During the service, the presence of three new couples in the small congregation was very noticeable. I just took it for granted that they were all from the same church.

After the service, one couple indicated that they were the people who had called me the night before. After a few minutes, out the door came the

Smiths and the Cornells, and after the introduction, it dawned on me that I had delegations from two vacant churches! I was a bit nonplussed. I had not applied to Chippawa Presbyterian Church—I was not even aware that it existed, let alone that it was vacant. Later that day as we sat talking with the Smiths and the Cornells, my wife, Diane, and I learned a little more about the church to which I was shortly to be called.

Since its first services in 1831, the church had, through the years, served Presbyterians living in and around the small village of Chippawa. Located not far from the city of Niagara Falls, and just upstream from the falls itself, the village had continued to maintain its own separate identity. During the mid-1950s, new subdivisions began to spring up around the old village core, and Chippawa eventually was incorporated into the city, but the older residents talked and acted as if it were still a small village.

During that period, the church experienced unprecedented growth. The old sanctuary was filled to capacity, and a second service was added. A modern sanctuary was built in 1960 and growth continued, peaking in 1964 with an average Sunday morning worship attendance of 185. Then followed 14 years of steady decline. Sunday school enrollment plummeted from 237 to 67, despite the erection of a new well-equipped Christian education wing and the hiring of a Christian education director. Sunday morning worship attendance dropped to 130. Then in 1978, the church suffered a series of demoralizing blows. Within months, first the organist, then the Christian education director, then the minister, and finally the church secretary resigned. Coupled with a shaky financial position, it left this long-established and rather traditional congregation severely shaken.

The Smiths and Cornells explained to me that the Chippawa congregation was looking for a recent seminary graduate who could help stem the decline and lead the church into a period of growth. They wanted someone who would be able to bring back to active involvement those members who had fallen away over the years, and at the same time attract new and younger families. That was to be their new minister's mandate.

On January 15, 1979, I was inducted as the minister of Chippawa Presbyterian Church. During the months that followed, I had an opportunity to observe the congregation. No new programs or innovations were attempted. My main concern was to get to know the people and try to pinpoint some of the root causes of the church's current problems. Innovations could come later. Looking back, I realize that this was a very poor strategy. Much valuable time during that "honeymoon" period, when a congregation is most receptive to change, was lost. The people came to know my leadership style as a rather passive one, and later, some found it hard to accept when that style changed.

As far as the course the church was following, things remained about the same as before I arrived.

15

It is said that a new broom sweeps clean, but such did not seem to be the case. Sunday morning worship attendance remained static and the finances continued on their shaky course. At one point the gas company threatened to shut off the gas because of a large outstanding bill. Despite having a new minister, morale was low. In talking with many members of the congregation, I noticed that most had all but given up hope that the negative trend could be reversed. It had become apparent to them that their expectation of attracting new members and reactivating old ones through a new young minister was not working out.

In desperation, I began to teach a ten-week church-growth course to the elders and anyone else who wished to come. I quickly discovered that interest in church growth was limited. Class attendance dropped from twenty-four the first week to eight at the final session. Many of the people were just plain apathetic; few were willing to take on responsibility of any kind. When I did get around to initiating anything new, the unspoken response seemed to be: "Sure, if you want to do the work, Pastor." Commitment was not a widely understood concept.

The study of church growth principles, with a faithful core of eight people, in some ways only served to heighten my frustration and perplexity.

We studied one chart which gave the following reasons people start to attend a certain church:

10 to 20 percent	come because of the pastor
3 to 8 percent	walk in off the street
4 to 10 percent	come because of a special program
3 to 4 percent	come because of a special need
.5 percent	come as the result of an evangelistic crusade
10 to 25 percent	were visited by church members
3 to 6 percent	come because of the Sunday school.

Most significant of all, though, a whopping 60 to 90 percent are *invited by friends, neighbors, or relatives.*

A Sunday morning survey of our own congregation showed that we had not taken in a new member in three years and that fully 70 percent of our people never had brought anyone to church who then became actively involved. There seemed to be little or no interest in personal evangelism of any kind. No wonder we had not experienced growth! The best mechanism for attracting people to the congregation was not operative. I became so depressed with the hopelessness of the situation that in less than a year after accepting the call, I was on the verge of resigning. I could see no way to turn the situation around.

Then one day while reading Robert Schuller's book *Your Church Has Real Possibilities,* I came across this statement, which rechanneled my thinking into a new and exciting direction: "We recommend a minimum of 5 percent of the church budget for publicity purposes."[1] This money was to be directed toward telling the people in a church's ministry area what the church can do for them. A quick calculation showed that only .6 percent ($300) of our proposed $50,000 budget for the coming year was allocated to advertising. It was a pittance. But just think what I could do if I had $2,500 to work with! That would permit me to advertise in a manner I was sure would have a significant impact on our community and our church.

As I considered the possibilities of this approach, I began to understand one of our fundamental problems. Members of the congregation prided themselves that theirs was a community-oriented church. This stemmed partly from the decision, made at the time of the erection of the new Christian education wing with gymnasium, that the church's facilities were not the exclusive property of the members, but were to be available for community use. The congregation felt that a community church should rent out its facilities to anyone who wants to use them—senior citizens, nursery schools, exercise groups, and so on. However, the church was not community-oriented in the sense that it established programs to meet the needs of the unchurched.

Actually, the congregation was introverted. Its programs were designed to meet the needs of members only. There were few active groups in the church other than Boy Scouts and Girl Guides, and those that were there existed basically for our own members. What people were accustomed to, and what most of them really wanted, was a mainte-nance-oriented ministry.

I came to the conclusion that our only hope was to redirect our efforts toward reaching the un-churched. After all, was that not one of the primary purposes for which the Church of Jesus Christ existed in the first place? There was only one reason a church would advertise, and that was to reach and attract those who had no church home. If it were interested only in maintaining existing structures, a church would not need to advertise. Its own members would already know that it existed and the content of its program. Because our people would not invite others to come to church, and if they would not (or could not) engage in personal evangelism, then adver-tising was the only avenue of outreach left open.

Enthusiastically I proposed at the annual meet-ing that we allocate 5 percent of the budget for the coming year to advertising. I spoke of our need to let our "light so shine before men" that they could see our "good works and give glory" to our "Father who is in heaven" (Matt. 5:16). There was little discussion about my proposal. The congre-gation voted overwhelmingly to give it a try. Actually, few understood the importance of the step we had taken and the impact it would have on the life of the church. If they had realized that the comfortable complacency of the past was about to be disturbed, I doubt that some members would have been so enthusiastic. To the credit of a good proportion of the congregation, it was a step

19

of faith. They had no idea where the money was to come from, and I had no idea just how I was going to spend the money—or more important, what kind of advertising I was going to do. This book is a result of that step of faith.

II

Why Advertise?

The first matter I had to explore was what advertising can (and cannot) accomplish. This is a basic question with which all advertisers, religious or secular, must come to grips. Advertising will not necessarily cause everyone to switch to your product or service immediately, but good advertising will do a number of things, depending upon the person who sees or reads the ad. In other words, there are three possible effects that good advertising can have on people, and the effect that results will be determined largely by what stage a person "is at" in his thinking. Advertising can:

1. stimulate impulses that are either dormant or repressed;
2. rechannel, redirect, and modify existing attitudes toward a product or service; or
3. persuade a person to try or sample a product or service for the first time.

When these effects are related to the church, we can see, first of all, what advertising will not do. It will not convert hard-core pagans to the Christian faith (or soft-core pagans, either, for that matter). It will not transform a community of effectively unchurched people into regular church attenders.

But this is what good, attractive, and imaginative copy will do:

1. *It will stimulate an interest in your church.* A church that advertises is obviously a church that has something to advertise, a church where something positive is happening. People are interested in hearing about an alive church.

   One of the members of Chippawa who agreed to do a testimonial ad told me that a great many people had mentioned to him that they were impressed with the kind of advertising our church had been doing. One man wrote to him:

   > Read about you in the local paper and your involvement in your church. It was a refreshing change from what we normally get and I thoroughly enjoyed it.

2. *It can stimulate thoughts and impulses* that may have lain dormant for years. Florence had not attended church in twenty years. Many times she had said to herself, "I must start back again . . . ," but she never got around to it. Then she began to notice our unusual ads in the general section of the paper. Thinking, "A church that advertises like that must be different," she came one Sunday to see what we were like . . . and she stayed.

3. *Advertising can serve as that positive first step* in persuading both unchurched people and those

dissatisfied with their past church affiliation to try your church, once. Jean and her husband Sam were relatively new in town. They had tried several churches, but were unhappy with what they had experienced. After reading an ad which described our contemporary and informal 9:30 service, Jean decided to "try us out." The next week she was back with her husband.

Advertising has made people aware of Chippawa Presbyterian Church in a way they had not been before. Oh, we had done the usual things that churches do to make their presence known. We had a traditional ad on the church page of our local newspaper. There was an inconspicuous sign on the front of the church. We were listed in the Yellow Pages, along with all the other churches. (That one was free!) Occasionally, there was an article about us in the newspaper. For example, there was the time the old church burned to the ground. A local reporter worked up quite a spread over that one.

In other words, we had done most of the things churches do, but people still did not know about us. I would guess that 75 percent of the population were not aware we were here. Our ad on the church page was indistinguishable from the conglomeration of other church ads. And besides, who reads the church page? Only church people—people who already were members of our church or of another church in town. Very poor prospects indeed!

Our church sign, while it was standing, had been designed for the horse and buggy age and was

23

rather dowdy. Few who passed by even noticed it, and from the vantage point of a car traveling at 50 kph (30 mph), it was unreadable. Worse still, when the sign deteriorated due to age, it was removed. For two years, the church was signless. One couple new to the community thought the church was without a minister and did not begin to attend until a new, eye-catching sign appeared.

Advertising has changed this apathy toward our church. People are now aware that Chippawa Presbyterian Church is alive and well and active. The church is talked about in the community in a positive sense—not because of a fire or a scandal. It is a rare Sunday when we do not have some new faces in our midst, people who are "trying us out." Some come back regularly, some join our church, others we may never see again. But that is not the fault of the advertising.

Those are some of the more significant and visible benefits that advertising can provide for a church. There are others, but we will touch on them later.

Are visitation and personal evangelism passé? Is advertising the modern-day answer to evangelism? The answer to both these questions is No. Actually, in respect to the personal evangelism versus advertising debate, I would suggest that we are not talking about an either/or, but a both/and situation.

Secular marketers do not speak in either/or terms, but of a *marketing*, or *promotional*, *mix*. This promotional mix would be made up of the following components:

1. *advertising*—any paid form of nonpersonal presentation and promotion of ideas, goods, or services by an identified sponsor;
2. *personal selling*—an oral presentation to prospective purchaser(s) with the intention of making a sale;
3. *publicity*—the stimulation of demand for a product or service by a favorable presentation of it through radio, television, or newspaper. Publicity may be solicited, but is not paid for;
4. *sales promotion*—any marketing activity other than the above which stimulates consumer demand. It may include such things as luncheons, trade shows, demonstrations.

In diagram form, the promotional mix in secular marketing looks like this:

The Promotional Mix Related to Consumer and Industrial Goods[1]

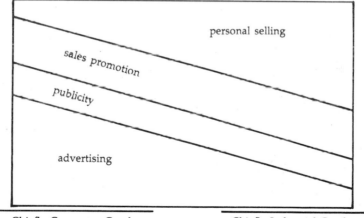

personal selling

sales promotion

publicity

advertising

Chiefly Consumer Goods   Chiefly Industrial Goods

This diagram shows that with certain consumer goods (e.g., soap or bread), little in the way of personal selling is required to move the product most of the time; with certain industrial goods, however, the emphasis on advertising will be low, and the company will depend almost entirely on its sales force to carry the promotional effort. Then of course there are those categories of both consumer and industrial goods (e.g., automobiles, word processors) which require a balance of both advertising and personal selling.

Moving from the secular to the sacred, the promotional mix diagram would look like this:

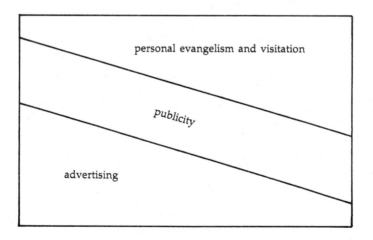

My contention is that churches need to establish a balance between personal word-of-mouth promotion and nonpersonal promotion. Just where that balance will be will depend upon each church's unique situation. In the past, the emphasis has been almost exclusively on the word-of-mouth approach. Little planning was involved, and quite frankly, the execution was haphazard at best.

Over the years many churches have used the canvasing-of-a-neighborhood approach, or door-to-door calls, to recruit new members. Extensive use of this technique has been made by the sects as well. This approach has the advantage of being a very personal form of communication. However, it has its disadvantages. One is the difficulty of recruiting and training volunteers. The other is the growing lack of cooperation on the part of the public with door-to-door solicitation of any kind. And in areas of high apartment concentration this type of visitation is almost impossible. Many door-to-door marketing programs are switching to direct-mail advertising.

Advertising will be increasingly required in a church's outreach program, to create awareness and to identify prospective new members who have indicated an interest in the church. Beyond this, advertising cannot go. It is then up to the individual church to arrange visitation and other programs to complete the process of leading these men and women to a personal commitment to Jesus Christ and to a desire to become responsible members of his Church.

III

Some Basic Advertising Principles

Let's begin with some sobering facts. A study done in the early 1960s indicated that the average adult was confronted by 560 or more advertising messages during every working day. More recent estimates place that figure at an astounding 1,500 to 1,700 messages. As we read the newspaper, watch prime-time television, listen to the car radio, open our mail, leaf through a magazine in the doctor's office, glance at billboards, write with a pen (from Joe's TV), pick up a book of matches, or gaze at transom ads during the bus trip home from the office, we are bombarded by 1,700 advertising messages.

Of those 1,700 daily messages, the average adult notices about 75. But of those 75 ads, only 10 or so will create a positive impression. Rather depressing, isn't it? Let's face it, your advertisements must work in a very competitive area. Some advertisers with whom you must contend for attention have spent hundreds of thousands of dollars on ad campaigns. What is more, they have been able to employ the expertise of some of the most creative minds in the business.

But before you toss out the idea because of the tremendous odds that your ads will never be read, consider the good news. The vast majority of advertising messages are junk and will not even be noticed. Either they are irrelevant, or so poorly conceived that they are not worth remembering. Besides, the majority of advertisements are directed at trying to create real or imagined differences among mass-packaged products that are essentially the same.

This book will help you create ads that will gain attention and be read; ads that will strike cords of responsiveness in the hearts of men and women; ads that aim, not at creating *wants,* but at meeting basic human *needs;* ads that will attract people to your church, where they can be exposed to the good news about our Lord and Savior Jesus Christ.

Gaining Attention

As should be obvious from our discussion so far, gaining attention is the name of the game. An ad that is not read or watched or listened to is a waste of time and money. To be effective, it must be noticed. There is an old story about a farmer who had a very stubborn mule that seemed to be untrainable. Finally, after numerous unsuccessful attempts, he called in a man who had considerable expertise in working with such animals and gave him the job of training the mule. The first thing the expert did was give the beast a stunning blow on the forehead with a stout board. The farmer protested against such

29

rough treatment—"I asked you to train my mule, not kill it!" The expert replied, "The first step in training a mule is to *get its attention!*"

To gain a reader's or listener's attention is the primary task of the church advertiser. And because our efforts are directed "to the glory of God," the results must be of the very highest order. We must give our best and most creative talents to the Master. Mediocrity is not acceptable.

I believe church advertising must be different, if it is to gain attention and be read. If it looks or sounds just like other advertising, it will fail. To be successful in fulfilling its intent, it must carry with it a sense of excitement, a disarming honesty and openness, and a stimulating intentionality that befits the most dynamic institution in the history of humankind.

In order to be noticed, our advertising must create a strong visual impact. Otherwise, a reader's scan will quickly pass to another article, ad, or page. The opportunity will have been lost and money wasted.

Keep It Simple

The KISS formula (Keep It Simple, Stupid) is one that applies to most areas of communication, but nowhere is it more important than in advertising. Many advertisers expend a great deal of effort to be either arty or witty. In their headlines and in the body copy of their ads, they try to employ words and sentence structures that carry subtle nuances of meaning. Unfortunately, such subtlety either

30

escapes most readers or it confuses them. And serious prospects are not interested in craftily conceived ads; they are more concerned with facts than adjectives and with specifics than generalizations.

An ad must be attention catching, but at the same time, its message must be simple, clear, and readily understood if it is to be grasped by the prospect. This means that layouts should be simple—one large picture, rather than three or four small ones; fact-filled headlines and body copy, written in clear, concise, readable language.

People have a tremendous tendency to be confused by even simple things. If a thing can be taken several ways, there is a certain percentage who will take it the wrong way every time. A safe rule of thumb: If the strategy or idea behind a particular ad is complicated, then it probably is a poor ad. If someone must read your whole ad to get the right message, then 80 percent of those who even notice your ad will get the wrong impression.

Watch Your Language

Examine the following headlines to see what you can learn about the products they promote. Keep in mind as you read them that out of every five people who notice an ad, four will read *only* the headline.

1. Initial impressions are lasting.
2. Pride and joy.
3. There's more to a great tomato sandwich than tomatoes.

31

4. Honour a Canadian Cow.
5. The more you look, the more you like.
6. Weekend Commuter.
7. It's tough to please a woman.
8. They don't grow on trees. But they'll grow on you.

  (1. whiskey; 2. automobile; 3. mayonnaise; 4. cheese; 5. automobile; 6. whiskey; 7. automobile; 8. yogurt)

The obvious conclusion is that while some of these headlines are attractive and even witty, they fail to carry an intelligible and easily understood message. They tell you little or nothing about the products they are trying to sell.

Now examine the next group of headlines, using the same criteria.

1. Fiat injects a little fun into driving. Try it—you'll love it.
2. Raid Insect Strip kills flies and mosquitoes, indoors, for up to four solid months.
3. If it'll store in your fridge or freezer, it should be in a Ziploc bag.
4. Opening a package of Mr. Christie's new soft cookies is like opening the oven door.

  (1. automobile; 2. insect strip; 3. food storage bags; 4. cookies)

You may not consider these ads gems of creative endeavor, but they communicate solid, intelligent, and relevant facts about the products. If you read only the headline (and that is all 80 percent of the people will read) you will learn what the product is and some relevant information about it. You will get the message. Two things should be noted about the last set of ads. The first is their clarity of language. The meaning is unmistakable. The second is their speed. The message is communicated quickly and succinctly.

The point I wish to make is this: The best way to get your message across in any advertisement is to come right out and say it. This is especially true of church advertising. Much of Christian communication is excessive verbage. Preachers are notorious for saying in twenty-five minutes what often could be said in five or ten. People find this confusing, just as they find complicated advertising confusing. If you want to get your message across, and at the same time get the most mileage out of your advertising dollar, then give it to them straight! Call a spade a spade! Your readers will appreciate it.

Be Creative, Not Strange

I have already made the point that church advertising must be different if it is to gain attention. By *different*, I mean that it must be outstanding, a cut above the ordinary. But by no means am I suggesting that it need be strange or bizarre.

Ads that are bizarre are different, and they may well attract attention, but it is doubtful that they would persuade people to attend your church unless they were looking for a sideshow. A minister wearing a halo, the ladies of the missionary society dancing in the aisles, upside-down copy, or a full page ad in black, with only the name of the church in big white letters—all would gain attention, but at the expense of losing your own credibility and your readers' respect.

By all means, use your God-given creative talents, but remember what you are trying to accomplish. Do not lose touch with reality in your efforts to be different and attract attention. Maintain an honesty and integrity that befits a servant of the King of Kings.

The Bottom Line

What determines whether an ad campaign is a success or a failure? In the secular world, that is an easy question to answer—*sales!* The ads may have been attractive and creative; they may have been widely read; but if they did not increase sales, then the campaign was a flop. Advertising is supposed to sell the product!

You might feel that such a pragmatic approach has no place in the church. But I think it does. True, we are not selling a product, so sales cannot be the determining criteria of a successful advertising campaign. But we do provide a service, and surely the measure of success of any service-oriented organization is the number of people who use the service. The measure of success for your church advertising campaign is Sunday attendance. That is

34

the bottom line. If your ads attract new people to your church, then they are successful. If they do not, your campaign is a flop.

Church attendance is the most sensitive measure of the health of a church. It will also serve as a gauge to check the degree of success of any change in program or church growth strategy. That is why our ushers count the attendance every Sunday morning. It permits me to tell statistically what is happening. For example, no new faces, but an increase in attendance means that my ads are stimulating interest among church members, but not among the unchurched. The presence of new faces, but a decline in average attendance points to the fact that a new program or approach may be stimulating to the unchurched, but that it is offending a number of the faithful.

However you choose to interpret the result, the bottom line is average Sunday attendance. If your ads fail to attract new people and increase attendance, reevaluate your advertising in a pragmatic manner. Don't hide behind excuses or rationalizations as to why your ads are not effective. Keep working at them until you come up with the best ads you are capable of producing. God has given you certain talents and gifts which he expects you to use to the very best of your ability. Don't stop striving until you have reached your fullest creative potential.

IV

Creating an Advertising Strategy

Advertising, like any other worthwhile endeavor, requires a planned strategy. If you fail to plan your strategy carefully, then you are planning to fail. A haphazard approach will lead to haphazard results. To make sure you are exercising wise stewardship over the advertising budget entrusted to you, be certain to take into consideration the various elements outlined in this chapter. A church advertiser should follow the wise guideline, "Plan your work and work your plan."

Describe Your Target (Exactly)!

I will be dealing with this subject of setting a target market again in chapter 5, from the standpoint of newspaper advertising. There I will make the point that our advertising should be aimed at the unchurched. In broad terms, I feel that they should be our market. But let us realize that this target probably accounts for 80 percent of the population in Canada and 60 percent in the United States. It is too broad a category to be workable. We might feel we would like to reach everybody within our church's ministry area, but it is just not possible. Not everyone is interested in the gospel of Jesus Christ, nor are they interested in his Church.

Furthermore, no one ad will have universal appeal. When you examine ads for products that are used by virtually everyone, you will notice that even those ads are designed to appeal to certain target groups that have the greatest sales potential. For example, ads for bread are designed to appeal to homemakers, who do the majority of the nation's grocery shopping and make the final decision about the brand to be purchased.

In the church, we often speak glibly of wanting to reach out to the community around us. The *community* is taken to be a geographical area and usually is described in terms of certain physical boundaries. Personally, I don't think a church can reach out to an entire community—*community* being the people in a certain geographical area. The reason for this is that most churches appeal only to certain groups of people. The groups might be categorized on the basis of socioeconomic status, musical preference, age, education, and so on. The people who make up these groups probably would prefer to go to a church that is frequented by people like themselves.[1] It is difficult to make them cross socioeconomic barriers. I am not saying that this situation is either right or wrong—it just happens to be the way things are.

For advertising to be successful, it must be specific. It is much easier to hit a distant target with a rifle than with a shotgun. A single well-aimed bullet is more effective than buckshot. The first question you must ask yourself is, Who do I want to reach with my advertising? Let us suppose you want to reach singles. That is a start in defining your target market, but it is still too broad. Consideration of the singles ministry of High Street United Methodist Church in Muncie, Indiana, will show the diverse categories into which singles can be further subdivided:

1. *New Day Group* (age concentration: 20s and up). This group has two phases. Phase 1 is for persons who are working through the initial trauma of separation and divorce (hurt, anger, etc.). Phase 2 is for those who, having worked through the initial adjustment, are ready for life to go on. It deals with such issues as single parenting, dating, remarriage, and other practical issues.

2. *TNTs—Twenties 'N Thirties*. This group is designed for young adults—college students or career persons who are single, or single again because of death or divorce.

3. *Christian Singles Fellowship* (age concentration: 35 and up). The purpose of this group is to meet the social and spiritual needs of Christian single adults by providing opportunities for personal and spiritual growth, for making new friends and developing relationships, for caring and sharing, for fun and fellowship.

4. *BYKOTA—Be Ye Kind One To Another* (age concentration: 40 and up). This is a weekly Bible

study support group, designed to assist singles
in spiritual growth and daily Christian living.

From this breakdown, you can see that to choose
"singles" as a target market is too broad a category.
Anyone reading your ad would wonder who is
being referred to. Aim your advertising at the
specific group you want to reach. Describe your
intended audience in precise terms. For example,
you might categorize them on the basis of
   age (over 30?)
   sex (female?)
   marital status (single, married with young
      children, retirees?)
   education (high school, college?)
   income ($20,000 + ?)
   musical preference (country and western,
      classical, folk?).

You should also keep in mind the family
members who are most likely to make the decision
as to whether, when, and where a family goes to
church. It would be wise to design your ads to
appeal to the predominant decision makers. For
instance, advertising for automobile tires is aimed
almost exclusively at a male audience and it almost
always appears in the sports section. The reason: It
is the rare wife who buys tires for the family chariot.
And at your house, when a decision is made to go
out to eat, who makes the final choice as to whether
it will be MacDonald's or Burger King? The fast food
restaurant operators have discovered that fre-

39

quently it is children who make that decision, and that is why they aim their promotions (free *Star Wars* glasses, balloons, etc.) at the youngsters.

Stress Benefits, Not Features

Much advertising stresses features—the mechanical attributes of a product. And most church advertising is feature-oriented.

Come to our old-fashioned Revival Hour.
Visit our Teen-and-Twenty Class.
Pastor Joe Smith preaching at both services.

Features are great, especially if they are unique to your church. They provide you with something around which to design your advertising.

People, however, are more interested in benefits than in features. A feature is meaningful to them only if it contains a benefit that will help them or that will have an impact on their lives. Your "old-fashioned revival hour" or "teen-and-twenty" group must have benefits, and those benefits must be clearly stated and stressed. Otherwise, there is no reason anyone should come. Many churches list in their ads that nursery care is provided. This is presented as a feature. To provide stronger copy, nursery care should be presented in terms of the benefits that accrue to the parents: Worship can be more enjoyable when parents do not have the hassle of children crawling all over them. Point out that they can worship with peace of mind, knowing that their children are being cared for "in our bright, spacious, and well-supervised nursery." Ten other churches in town may advertise that nursery care is provided but it would not be hard for a young family to see the benefits of your nursery over and above all others.

The Big Idea

Your advertising should stress one large central theme, if it is to catch people's imagination. If it does not contain what one advertising mogul calls *the big idea*, it will pass by your audience like a ship in the night.

Why Bother with a Campaign?

In much of what we have mentioned so far and will deal with in more detail later, the emphasis focuses on single ads. This might prompt you to wonder whether it is necessary to worry about devising a campaign. Why not develop a series of creative ads and let each one go it alone?

But such an approach is unwise. In the first place, a series of single ads, each taking off in a different creative direction, would be confusing to your audience. People grasp unified advertising, built around a single theme, or *big idea*. Advertising must be recognized. Your audience must be comfortable with it. Only when your advertising becomes recognized will it begin to pay dividends.

Moreover, both the cost and the time required to come up with new ads which aim in different

41

creative directions would be prohibitive. With a campaign, there is no need for the advertiser to create, design, and test a number of new ideas for each ad. It allows time to concentrate on better ways to communicate the same idea.

If you want your advertising to be effective, plan a campaign—a good, well-planned campaign will last for years. Some in the secular world have run for fifteen or twenty years and still maintain their effectiveness.

The essential distinguishing feature of a campaign is *commonality,* or similarity. At least one of the following elements must be present if a series of ads is to constitute a campaign.

1. *A Common Look.* A common look, or visual similarity, can be achieved in a number of ways. You can use the same format, or layout, in each ad, changing only the details. You can use the same kind of type for headlines and for body copy in all the ads. You might present a demonstration that never varies, or a testimonial format that changes only by using different people. You can consistently use the same spokesperson or announcer. Resemblance also can be achieved through similarly styled artwork or graphic design. It is important to develop a visual style that your audience can identify and become familiar with.

2. *A Common Sound.* Of course, this would apply only to radio or TV. It could be achieved by one distinctive sound—a train whistle, the ringing of a doorbell or a telephone; or by a unique

voice—deep baritone, husky, or very soft; or by a catchy tune or musical jingle. Again, the important thing is to develop a sound style that people can identify.

3. *A Common Outlook, or Philosophy.* The aim here is attitudinal similarity. This might be an attempt to express the philosophy of your church—to create a church image. The image might be of a warm, friendly church; a Bible-believing church; a socially concerned church; a people-centered church; a dynamic, exciting church. It is doubtful if you could build a campaign on the basis of common outlook or attitude alone, but it can give a campaign based on a common look or sound an additional kick and effectiveness.

It must be remembered that what you want to create through a campaign is a basic resemblance that can be recognized. Do not take it too far, however, by producing identical twins.

Timing a Campaign

It would be tremendous if you could keep your church's message before the public on a continuously high level throughout the entire year. If money were no object, this would be an excellent strategy. Unfortunately, it is beyond the financial capability of most congregations.

There are two alternatives in terms of scheduling advertising. The first is known as *flighting*. Using this approach, an advertiser concentrates on certain times of the year, but does no advertising whatever in the intervals between those times. The following Gallup Poll chart would be useful to the church advertiser wishing to employ a flighting strategy.

Seasonal Fluctuations in Church Attendance 1955–1977[2]

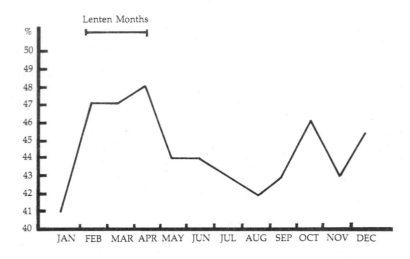

If your strategy is based on the theory that one should advertise when people are in the buying mood, then your advertising should be concentrated on those periods of the year when people are most willing to attend church. This would mean scheduling three flights of high-level advertising:

1. *during Lent,* a month before Easter;
2. *during September,* as the new school year begins; and
3. *during the month of December,* leading up to Christmas.

Flighting is useful for a church with a very limited advertising budget, but it ignores an important fact. Successful advertising requires frequency. Because people forget quickly, your ads must be kept before the audience on a regular basis. Moreover, a frequently scrutinized ad helps them retain your message.

A better strategy would be *pulsing.* Diagrammatically, it would look like this:

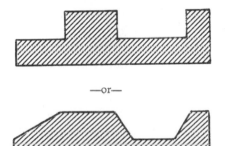

—or—

Pulsing permits at least a low level of advertising on a continuous basis. It allows you to keep your church's name before the public with regularity. It also permits you to advertise at a high level during those times of the year when people are most likely to go to church.

Well, What Did You Expect?

I do not know what response you will expect from your first attempt at advertising, but I remember very well what I expected from my first campaign. In a church that could seat 275 people, and where attendance over the past year had averaged 130, I hoped to have overflow crowds at both services on Easter Sunday morning. The campaign was a one-week blitz that gobbled up one-quarter of my advertising budget. I had prepared and sent out a mass mailing of 9,000 pieces and had supplemented that with several newspaper ads.

The result? Well, it wasn't exactly what I had expected. We had about 265 people for the two services. As I look back, I can see that I broke just about every advertising principle that I am trying to elucidate in this book. But at least it was a start.

What you must realize is that advertisng is not a miracle solution that will change your attendance overnight. To be effective, advertising requires a sustained effort over a long period of time. If you have done your homework properly in terms of preparing a campaign, then you will see results in the short run, but they will not be dramatic results. Only as you invest in advertising as a long-range strategy will you see it having a significant impact on your church's attendance.

Let me give you an illustration from the secular world that will help clarify the long-range nature of advertising. Oneida Silversmiths did some pioneer work in the area of advertising. Oneida, up until the turn of the century, had marketed a very low quality silverware. In 1902, a decision was made to turn to the manufacture of quality flatware and to embark on the then uncharted waters of national advertising in order to establish a strong acceptance of the new product by the consuming public. The step was taken with the knowledge that it would be a number of years before sales of the new product increased enough to pay for the massive amount of advertising necessary to gain national acceptance. In actuality, it was eight years before sales were sufficient to cover the costs. Eventually, after having established a national position for Oneida Community Plate, advertising was confined to a reasonable percentage of sales.

From this example, we can draw two important points.

1. Advertising is a long-term, long-range strategy, not a one-shot effort. Once begun, an organization must continue to advertise as long as it is in business.
2. It takes a large initial investment to become known to the public. The reason the vast majority of church advertising is ineffective is that too little of it is done, at too infrequent intervals.

Also, remember that advertising is only one part of your church's marketing mix. For the most part, advertising can only persuade people to try your church once. If they do not like what they see or

47

hear or experience, they won't be back. If advertising increases the number of first-time visitors to your church, but you never see them again, then do not blame the advertising. To twist an old adage, "Good advertising only makes a sick church die more quickly."

V

Building a Church Image

The idea of building an image for a church contains overtones of Madison Avenue and is viewed skeptically by many clerics. *Creating an image* is seen as being manipulative, and the contention is that such a device has no place in a church. I heartily disagree with such shallow reasoning. Everything a church does tends to create an image. And I mean everything, including the architectural style of the building, the way the grounds are kept, the greeters at the door (or lack of them), the type of music, the style of a church sign, and the order of service—to name only a few. So it is not a matter of debating whether creating an image is right or wrong. The only applicable question is whether a church wants to create a positive image, or a negative image.

Now there are two schools of thought in regard to this business of a church's image. One school says that your advertising and publicity must tell it like it is. In other words, your church must be what it claims to be. If you say you are a friendly church, then people who come to visit better find you friendly, or they will charge you with false advertising and "bad mouth" you all over town. I agree with this school of thought, but only to a certain point. What about the poor little church that has been on a "downer" for ten or twenty years? If that church must tell it like it is, then there is no point in advertising.

There is, however, a second way to look at image-creation. I call it creating a *faith image*. It is based upon the great biblical definition of faith found in Hebrews 11:1, "Now faith is the assurance of things hoped for, the conviction of things not seen." The old adage, Seeing is believing! delineates the realm of doubting Thomases, but it should have no place in the thought-life of those of us who are servants of the Most High. As men and women of vision, our motto should be, rather, Believing Is Seeing! In other words, there is no need for you to be bound by the present image of your church, especially if that image is an unfavorable one. Reach out, and by faith, become the church that you believe God is calling you to be and intends you to be!

A church is very much like an individual. An individual becomes whatever the person perceives himself or herself as being. If he sees himself as being awkward around people and a bit of a "klutz," then he will become just that. If she perceives herself as being a warm and loving person, then that is what she will become. People who see themselves as being failures will never rise above that perception to become successful in life until they change their self-image. As long as they say to themselves, "I get all the bad breaks in life. I am a failure," they will be failures. And nothing will change their being failures—not even a series of good breaks—because their attitude is a negative one. They would not be able to accept a good opportunity if it came along. Only when these people develop a positive mental attitude and self-image will they progress from failure to success.

In the same way, a church never will become more than it perceives itself to be. If a church (and by that I mean the members) perceives itself as being cold and unfriendly, then that is the way it will come across to visitors. If a church sees itself as being a failure in ministry and outreach, it will have developed a mind-set that prevents it from attracting new people. This is why it is often so hard to turn around a church that has experienced an extended period of decline. But it is not impossible.

Let me give you an example. As the new minister of Chippawa Presbyterian Church, there was a point in my ministry when I had become very discouraged about the church's lack of growth and progress. After one year, we were still experiencing decline. My desire was for a progressive church that would reach out and touch the lives of people with the love of Jesus Christ. But it was not happening. We were dead on our feet, minister included. I *felt* that I was a failure, and as a result I *was* a failure.

It was at this point that I began to understand the faith-image concept. I reasoned that if faith was the "assurance of things hoped for, the conviction of things not seen," then God was calling me to look at my church, not as it was, but as it could be under him. And so in my mind's eye, I began to think of Chippawa Presbyterian Church in a new way. I looked, not at what it was, but at what I believed God wanted it to be. As I did this, a very positive image began to evolve in my mind. I began to perceive a dynamic church; a church with a very positive message, which would stimulate and inspire; a church that would serve as an encouraging inspiration to all who entered its doors. But I did more than just think of the church in those terms. I began to speak of it and preach about it and advertise it as such. At every available opportunity, I described it as exciting, stimulating, progressive, dynamic—"A Church for People on the Grow." In actuality, our church was not as I perceived it through the eyes of faith. But it is becoming what I believe God wants it to be. It was not long before I began to feel, within the church itself, a growing sense of excitement about what God was doing in our midst. Seeing is believing, you say? That is a losing attitude and the very antithesis of faith. No, Believing is Seeing! That is what it's all about, and that is what a *faith-image* is.

VI

Developing Newspaper Ads That Work

Now it is time to get down to specifics, and the most realistic place for you to begin is with newspaper advertising. Chances are that you already run a small weekly ad in your local paper. Newspaper is a familiar medium of communication and a not-too-threatening one in which to work.

Newspapers are economical and flexible. You can use as little or as much space as you can afford. Space is usually sold by the column inch. A column is usually about one and three-quarter inches wide. I like to use an ad that is three columns wide and seven inches long. I use this size for several reasons. It is large enough to be easily seen; but more important, it provides adequate space so that the ad appears uncluttered even though it contains a picture and a significant amount of body copy.

Defining Your Target Market

Your *target market* is that group or sector of the population you want to reach with your advertising. It is the first thing you must decide on when planning a campaign. It not only will determine the design and layout of your ads, but their location in the paper, and even in what newspaper you advertise.

I would guess that 95 percent of church advertising has for its target market other church people. How can I tell? Well, it is very simple. Where do most churches advertise? On the church page, along with all the other churches. They use catchy sermon titles to attract attention:

Greater Love

In the Midst of a Dry and Weary Land

Face to Face in One Place

New Wine for Old Wineskins

The Meanest Mother in the World

God's Wonderful Lovers

The Exposure of the Heart in the Expression of a Desire

Many Things in Parables

After studying the average religion page, I can only conclude that these ads are designed for church people, because they would be unintelligible to anyone else. The lingo used is for the "in" crowd and it is doubtful that the average man on the street would care much about "The Exposure of the Heart in the Expression of a Desire."

Now, far be it from me to tell you who your target

market should be. That is something every church must decide for itself. However, I can't help feeling that it is wrong to try to attract people who are satisfied with their own church. It is simply reshuffling the deck of the faithful. Why should we be vying to turn Methodists into Episcopalians or Presbyterians into Baptists, when well over half the population never darkens the door of *any* church. The brand-switching type of advertising (trying to get people in one church to switch to another) that most churches do is unworthy of the Church of Jesus Christ. If they are not trying to attract other church people, why advertise on the religion page? Not only are the ethics of such advertising questionable, it does not work—the religion page is the least-read page in any newspaper.

So my advice is to avoid the religion page like the plague. To advertise there is to throw your money away. It is a great deal for the newspaper, but it is a bust as far as your church is concerned. Instead, use what is known as *run-of-the-paper* advertising: Your ads are placed in the general news section, the sports section, the family section, and other parts of the paper. One Sunday morning, I conducted a simple survey. The previous week, I had run two ads—one in the general news section and one on the religion page. I asked people to indicate by a show of hands whether they had seen the ads. More than three-quarters of the congregation had seen the ad in the general news section, even though we had never advertised there before. But less than one-quarter had noticed the one on the religion page, and it was the most noticeable ad on the page. I will let you draw your own conclusions.

I feel strongly that church advertising should be directed to the effectively unchurched—to those who have no active involvement with a church, even though, if asked, they might say, "Oh, I'm a Lutheran, I guess. I had a great aunt who took me to a Lutheran church once. I guess that makes me a Lutheran." Jesus said that he came to call not the righteous, but sinners to repentance. If the effectively unchurched were his target market, should it not, in broad outline, be ours? For that reason, I try to design ads that will impress the unchurched.

Now, it is possible to subdivide your target market even further. If you want to reach men, think in terms of the business section or the sports section. If it is women you want to attract, then the women's, or family section, is a good bet. I like the general news section because I feel it gives our ads the broadest exposure for our advertising dollar. More people read that section than the special interest sections. But if you have something of exclusive interest to men or to the sports-minded, then by all means aim for the sports section.

It is possible that your newspaper may require you to pay a premium, or the regular commercial rate for run-of-the-paper advertising. The special church rate is usually reserved for the religion page. Believe me, it is worth the extra money to place your ads where they will be read. But don't be afraid to exercise a little holy boldness and ask that the paper charge you only the church rate. Charges usually are for space only, no matter how much copy you use, or whether photographs or drawings are included.

One further way to subdivide your target market is by selecting the newspaper in which you place your advertisements. Most churches have several options. First, there are the large dailies. In major centers there will be two or more—a morning paper, an evening, and others. Each appeals to a different segment of the population. For example, the city of Toronto has three daily newspapers. The *Globe and Mail* is a morning paper with a very literate audience. It is widely read by the business community and is, in a sense, almost a national paper. The other morning paper is *The Toronto Sun*. It is not delivered, but purchased at the newsstand by people on their way to work. This tabloid appeals to a younger and not too literate audience. The paper is often read only briefly and then passed on to someone else. *The Toronto Star* is an evening paper with a broad mass audience, read at a more leisurely time of day and more in depth than, for instance, *The Sun*. Your choice of newspaper will help you target your market. As far as readership of your ad is concerned, an evening paper is probably a better bet, although this is a generalization and would vary from area to area. Large-circulation dailies will give you broad coverage, but they also are expensive.

One way to reduce the cost is to advertise in one of the eight or ten special community editions published by many daily papers in large metropolitan areas. These editions usually have a section in which advertising rates are lower than in those sections that are delivered to the whole city. Check with the newspaper advertising departments to see what cost reducing suggestions they can make for you.

Possibly a community or neighborhood newspaper would be a better and more economical alternative for some churches. Rather than broadcasting your ads over an entire city, you would be able to zero in on one particular area. Advertising rates for community or weekly newspapers are lower than for dailies; and studies have shown that they remain in a home for a much longer period of time.

Another avenue worth pursuing is the local weekly shopper's news that is distributed without charge by large chain stores, supermarkets, and others. You might find that such ads are free—but it is doubtful.

One final consideration is the day of the week on which you should run your ad. Again I will be dealing in generalizations, since readership and circulation patterns vary from region to region. There does not seem to be a clear-cut concensus on this matter, but in Canada, at least, the two days with the largest circulation appear to be Wednesdays and Saturdays. Wednesday usually has a 10 to 15 percent increase over the other weekdays, and the reason is readily apparent. The Wednesday-night paper is widely read by women looking for specials at supermarkets and other stores. One problem with advertising on Wednesday is that your ad will have a tendency to get lost in the mass, unless it's outstanding. The circulation of the special weekend paper in places like Toronto and Montreal is 15 to 20 percent above that of an average weekday. As far as home delivery goes, some people take only the weekend edition, for the colored supplement and other special articles. Readership of these papers is high, but sometimes they are not read until Sunday afternoon (or later). The poorest night of the week, in terms of readership, is Friday. Papers still go into the homes, but readership is low. There are just too many other things to do on Friday night.

The season of the year also affects newspaper readership and circulation. Holiday time—especially summer holidays—significantly reduces the size of circulation and cuts into readership even more.

Eight Ways to Design Effective Ads

1. Put Your Message in the Headline

The most important element in print advertising (newspapers, magazines, etc.) is the headline. Research has shown that for every five readers your ad attracts, four will get no further than the headline. That means that only one person out of five will read the body copy. If you depend on that copy to carry your message, you will waste 80 percent of your advertising dollar.

So make sure that the key elements of your message are in the headline; and that includes your church's name, if possible. Consider the following hypothetical ad, which would be based on a picture of actor George Burns, who played God in the movie *Oh, God!*

(headline)

WE DON'T PLAY GOD . . .

(picture)

(body copy)

but we can introduce you to him. Come and worship him this Sunday, with some of the other members of his family.

9:30 A.M. or 11:00 A.M.

YORK PARK COMMUNITY CHURCH

Now, considering that 80 percent of the people will read no farther than the headline, the message they get will be this:

WE DON'T PLAY GOD

This is what is known as a *blind* headline. It tells the reader nothing. A headline should be able to stand on its own, apart from photographs, artwork, and body copy. A revised attempt at this ad may not be the last word in artistic creativity, but it will do what advertising is meant to do in a much better fashion.

(headline)

AT YORK PARK COMMUNITY CHURCH
WE DON'T PLAY GOD . . .
BUT WE CAN INTRODUCE YOU TO HIM!

(picture)

(body copy)

Come and worship him this Sunday with some of the other members of his family. . . .

9:30 A.M. or 11:00 A.M.

---

2 Use the Headline to Single Out Your Prospects

Let us suppose that your prospects are the parents of children up to the age of about twelve. You should design your headline to appeal to the self-interest of people in this market segment. Consider this headline:

CHIPPAWA PRESBYTERIAN CHURCH
HAS GREAT NEWS FOR THE PARENTS OF
PRESCHOOL & YOUNGER SCHOOL-AGE
CHILDREN!

Then in the body copy, describe a service which has been designed with the needs of young married couples in mind:

> a contemporary, informal worship service which runs concurrently with a church school program and nursery care.

3. Use Fact-filled Headlines

Common sense would suggest that short, catchy headlines are best. Research indicates otherwise. Well-written, long, fact-filled headlines sell more merchandise in the secular world. And when we consider that the children of darkness are wiser in many ways than the children of light, we in the church should take a leaf from their book. So don't be afraid of a headline that runs twenty or more words, if it tells your whole story.

4. Keep Your Headlines Positive

Remember, the gospel of Jesus Christ is good news! In fact, it is the best news. So make sure that the general tone of your ad, and the headline in particular, are positive. The human mind has a tendency to remember only the negatives. Do not give your readers that opportunity. The following ad was designed around a photograph of a typical suburban family getting into their car to take off on a weekend jaunt.

(headline)

NO TIME FOR CHURCH?

(picture)

(body copy)

Of course you do! You can make time!
Plan to be with us this Sunday.

What is wrong with this ad? First, the headline is
blind. It cannot stand by itself and it tells the reader
nothing. Second, it carries a negative message.
Anyone who reads it is going to agree with the
message—"That's right! I have no time for church"
—and flip to the next page. The advertiser who uses
an ad like this is paying to discourage people from
coming to his church. Rewritten in positive terms,
the headline might read:

OF COURSE YOU HAVE AN HOUR TO COME TO
CHIPPAWA PRESBYTERIAN CHURCH
THIS SUNDAY

5. Where Possible, Use Photographs

People notice a photograph before they notice a
drawing, and they remember it longer. So if at all
possible, use photographs in your ads, especially
those that have story appeal and will draw the

63

reader to the headline and, it is to be hoped, the body copy. Captions under photographs have a high readership, too; they are ads in their own right.

6. Long Body Copy Is Read by Prospects

Casual prospects lose interest after the headline; if the message is not in the headline, they are not interested. But people who read the body copy are serious prospects. And serious prospects want all the information you can give them. For instance, if a person is not interested in buying a car, then the only part of the car ads that will be read are the headlines. But if the family hack is getting sort of rough and a prospect is beginning to think about a new one, when a car ad is read, the body copy will be read, too. And the prospect will want all the facts—gas mileage, engine size, body style, and so on. So in your church ad, give the serious prospect facts, facts, facts. For an example, see Figure 2. Don't be scared off by long body copy. Aim at clarity, accuracy, factualness; and be specific.

7. Overall Impressions Are Important

Most church advertisers try to pack too much information into too small a space. The ad is either crammed with microscopic print or bloated with loud, screaming headlines, and the result is an ad with a cluttered appearance. Aim at simple layouts that create a good overall impression. This means one large photograph, rather than three or four small ones, and type and layout that will leave adequate white space.

8. Each Message Should Be Complete in Itself

Few of those who notice several of your ads will read all of them. *That's why it is important* that each ad be a complete message that can stand on its own. If only one ad out of a series of six is read, the prospect still will have gotten the essential message.

Figure 1

**Steve Dunkin, minister of dynamic,
people centred Chippawa Presbyterian Church**

The most important person at Chippawa Presbyterian Church is <u>YOU!</u>

That's right. In fact, we have designed our whole program with you in mind.

Take Sunday morning, for instance. We know that people have different tastes in worship and different needs. So we give you a choice of time and worship style.

Our 9:30 service is particularly suited to parents with young children. For tots under 3, special care and a simple program are provided in our bright, modern, and well equipped nursery. Our church school provides instruction in the Bible for those from age 4 to 14.

This leaves you free to enjoy the contemporary informality of this service. Music, under the enthusiastic leadership of our pianist Judy Sibley, ranged from well known hymns of the faith to contempoarry pieces. The message is designed to offer you the dynamic encouragement you need for successful living. The topics we cover are things you face every day. The principles we share will help you approach life in a hopeful winning way.

Our 11:00 a.m. is for you if a later hour is more convenient and a traditional approach to worship more meaningful. Nursery care is provided, as well as a special program for children aged 3 to 7.

Our concern is for people who want to grow in every area of life. We want to provide you with the encouragement, the inspiration, and the stimulation you need to become all that God intended and created you to be.

But then, don't take our word for it. Come, visit us this Sunday morning, and experience it for yourself.

CHIPPAWA PRESBYTERIAN CHURCH
8280 Willoughby Dr., Niagara Falls
A church for people on the grow!

Figure 2

Walt Baker, family man and elder of
Chippawa Presbyterian Church

We care about people at Chippawa Presbyterian Church

Chippawa Presbyterian Church has special meaning for me and my family. This has been our church home for over 31 years. Our three daughters have experienced the joy of belonging here throughout their childhood and teen years.

My life is centred around my home and family, my friends and my employment. But there is part of me that needs the church as I grow in my relationship with Jesus as my Saviour.

It is encouraging to see our church reaching out and people coming to hear the faith building messages which are helpful in the everydayt problems of life.

Enthusiasm is growing! As a result of a workshop held recently there is a deeper concern for meeting the needs of the people of our church and our community.

Why not visit us this Sunday and discover the positive Christian fellowship our church offers.

9:30 Contemporary and informal service, with children cared for in our bright, modern nursery and church school.

11.00 Traditional worship with children's service included.

Chippawa Presbyterian Church

8280 Willoughby Drive,   Niagara Falls

A Church for people on the grow!

Figure 3

Figure 4

Mrs. Judy Sibley, our enthusiastic organist and choir director.

At Chippawa Presbyterian Church, we believe in giving you a choice.

Music plays an important part in Worship at Chippawa Presbyterian Church. We know that not everyone likes the same type of music and so we provide a variety.

The 9:30 service gives you a chance to raise your voices in familiar choruses or try more modern music. This is an informal service featuring "Pick your own" Hymn sings which are a favourite of the congregation. The use of the piano at our 9:30 service provides a change from the organ.

Our 11 o'clock service provides the more traditional type of music. Our choirs lead in the singing of hymns and provide a musical selection each week. With traditional organ accompaniment familiar hymns of the church are sung.

At Chippawa Presbyterian church we want you to participate in the type of worship service that you feel comfortable with. So come and share with us in the inspirational service of your choice.

Judy Sibley

Chippawa Presbyterian Church

8280 Willoughby Drive,   Niagara Falls

A Church for people on the grow!

Figure 5

Figure 6

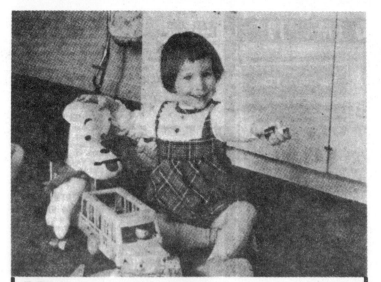

Figure 7

Figure 8

VII

Direct Mail—The Best Bet for Your Advertising Dollar?

Picture the following:

It is 5:30 P.M. and Joe Allen has just pulled into the driveway after a long day at Cross-Town Industries. He enters the house and, after depositing his briefcase or lunch box on the floor, calls out:

Hi, honey, I'm home.

After several minutes of chitchat, he asks that inevitable question:

Any mail today?

This little scenario is reenacted in millions of homes every working day of the year. It indicates one important thing. People are very interested in what comes to them through the mail.

This observation is supported by a recent Roper survey which polled 2,000 adults, asking them which of a series of daily events and activities they most looked forward to. There were 21 events and

74

activities on the list. In first place was "checking to see what you got in the mail"; 63 percent responded that this was something they anticipated with pleasure every day. In second place was time spent on special interests and hobbies, while watching a favorite television program came third.

The world of business has long understood the human desire to receive mail and the potential of mail in terms of marketing. Beginning with the pioneers of the industry, Eatons and Montgomery Ward, sales have grown to the point where they now exceed $80 billion a year in North America. In recent years, even some industrial giants have moved in to get a share of this lucrative market.

The first type of mail at which we wish to look is called *mass mail*. This type mail is not addressed to an individual, but to "Occupant," and usually is delivered to every householder living in a particular postal area. It is bulk mail (fliers, brochures, etc.), and the post office usually charges much less than the normal second-class mail rate. It has deservedly been given the name of junk mail. Frequently such mailings end up in the wastebasket without even being opened, let alone read. The response rate that your church could expect from such mailings is very low, ranging from .2 percent at best, down as far as .05 percent. This means that on a mailing of 1,000 pieces, you could expect one or two responses. To send out a mass mailing requires a lot of work for a negligible result. I do not recommend it for your church.

The second type of mail is *direct mail,* and I feel it

holds much greater potential as a tool which can be effectively utilized by a church to inform people in its ministry area about its programs and services. Direct mail is addressed to an individual and is sent either first or second class. The response rate that you can reasonably expect is as high as 1 to 3 percent.

The reasons for the popularity of the direct-mail marketing approach are many, and some, such as the increased cost of gasoline and the inconvenience for working women of shopping in retail stores, have little interest for the church advertiser. However, three qualities of direct-mail advertising make it a very advantageous medium for churches:

> selectivity
> predictability
> accountability.

Selectivity is the process of picking out a certain item or items from among a larger group. In buying apples, if one were being selective, one would buy a certain grade of Granny Smiths, for example, rather than a hodgepodge bushel of every type and size, in varying degrees of ripeness. In advertising, selectivity is the ability to direct your ad at a specific target market. Direct mail is highly selective. An advertiser can aim his appeal at people in a certain geographical area—covering whole sections of a city, or just one side of a street. Using a mailing list purchased from a list broker, the advertiser can send mailings to people with certain interests (health foods, sports, model railroads, etc.). This exactness is rarely found in other media. It is a good example of using a single rifle shot, rather than a shotgun approach, to hit a target.

Predictability means that with direct mail, because of past experience by other advertisers using this media, a certain level of response can be predicted for your mailing. This is not to say that the program or service you have to offer and the design of your direct-mail piece will have no effect on your letter's pulling power. Testing two letters that are identical, except for the first paragraph, may well demonstrate that one letter has a 50 percent greater response rate than the other. But the response rate for your mailing still will be within a predictable range.

The novice direct-mail advertiser would send out possibly 1,000 letters to a geographical area surrounding his church. His thinking typically would be something like this: "If only 10 percent respond to our invitation, we'll pack the church on Easter Sunday morning. And who knows, maybe we'll get more than that!" This is wishful thinking. On the basis of industry-wide experience, the predictable response to a piece of direct mail sent first class is somewhere between 1 and 3 percent, with 1 to 2 percent being more normal. Our friend who sent out 1,000 invitations can expect to see somewhere between 10 and 20 new faces on Easter Sunday as a result of his mailing. That would be a normal response—30 newcomers would be phenomenal!

Finally, there is *accountability*. The principles of direct-mail advertising have been firmly established

77

by mail-order advertisers. David Ogilvy, founding father of Ogilvy and Mather, the fifth largest ad agency in the world, is a strong advocate of direct-mail advertising. In his *Confessions of an Advertising Man,* he has this to say about direct-mail advertisers:

> This elite corps . . . knows more about the *realities* of advertising than anybody else. They are in a position to measure the results of every advertisement they write. . . . The mail-order advertiser has no retailers to shrink and expand their inventories, to push his product or to hide it under the counter. He must rely on his advertisements to do the entire selling job. Either the reader clips the coupon or he doesn't. A few days after his advertisement appears, the mail-order writer knows whether it is profitable or not.[1]

This holds true as well for the church advertisers who use direct mail. Not only can they learn from the tried and proven methods of designing and writing a direct-mail piece, they can know within a very short time what kind of response they will have. If the letter was an invitation to a Family Life Seminar, the advertiser will know exactly how many pink registration cards (sent out with the mailing) have been returned. If the offer was a free book on positive thinking (or faith) and a visit to explain more about the church, then the response rate will be known by the number of "Please send me . . ." cards that come back in the mail. Response to an invitation to attend your church is harder to estimate, unless your prospect is asked to fill out a card and bring it along. Direct mail also permits the advertiser to determine the cost of reaching one individual.

The objective when using direct mail is threefold:

1. to persuade the prospect to open your letter;
2. to persuade the prospect to read your letter;
3. to persuade the prospect to act on what your letter asks him or her to do.

This may sound simple and logical, but it can be quite a challenge.

Motivating People to Open Your Mail

The major hurdle is just inducing the prospect to open your letter. Most of us receive advertising mailings weekly and probably read very little of it. I know that unless it is about a product or service that I am vitally interested in, I usually toss such mail in the trash without even opening the envelope.

Direct mail is better than mass mail, but it is still impersonal. Anything you can do to personalize it will increase the chances of your letter being opened and read. Remember that your church is not in the junk mail business, pushing everything from pens to portable radios. Rather, you can offer people a program or service that can have a major impact for good on their lives. You are not motivated by a desire for profit, but by a concern for each person and his or her welfare. These concerns and motives should be expressed by making your church's mailing as personal as it possibly can be. There are several ways to make the envelope more personal and, at the same time, increase the number of people who will open it to read the letter.

1. Send your letter first class, and maybe even use a commemorative stamp. It costs a few cents more, but that is a small price to pay to have your letter opened. Second- or third-class postage, along with "Printed Matter" stamped on the envelope, is the kiss of death for any mailing.

2. Rather than placing the name of your church on the upper left hand corner of the envelope, use the name and address of one of your church members who is part of the sponsoring group for the advertised program. This person should be the one sending the mailing and his or her signature should appear on the letter as well.

3. Make sure the prospect's name is either hand-written or typed on the envelope. Do not stick on reproduced labels that give your mailing an impersonal look. Your aim is to send out a mailing that is personal mail—the kind you like to receive; the kind that makes you curious when you take it out of the mailbox.

4. If you send out regular mailings, place each one in a different color or different shape envelope. Remember, in direct mail, familiarity breeds contempt.

One final item might have a bearing on whether or not your letter will be opened—the day your mailing is sent out. Your letter has a greater opportunity to be looked at if it arrives on a low-volume mail day. Avoid the first and the fifteenth of the month—those are the dates bills are usually sent out. Try to time your mailing to arrive on a Tuesday, which is a low-volume mail day.

Motivating People to Read Your Mail

The next hurdle is to persuade the prospect to read your letter. Again, the very best advice I can give you is, Make it personal. If I receive a form letter that has been run off on an antiquated duplicator, and the salutation reads "Dear Friend," I am strongly tempted not to read it. However, I have never in my life *not* read a letter addressed to me personally. "Dear Steve" or "Dear Mr. Dunkin" has a magical quality that makes me want to read on. I may not like what I read, but I read it nevertheless.

Motivating People to Respond

Before you start to write your letter, there are several things you must decide. The approach I am going to suggest is really the only sensible and logical way to go about designing a direct-mail piece. Unfortunately, the temptation to just sit down and start writing is often overwhelming. But put the following points down on paper *before* you start drafting your letter.

1. *Your Aim or Objective.* You must know what you want to accomplish through your mailing. As I have pointed out, aim at reducing your objective to one big idea. This will clarify your thinking

and make it easier for the prospect to grasp the main thrust of your letter.

2. *Your Appeal or Offer.* Remember that the people in your target market will probably be very different from your regular church members. Make sure it is the needs of your target audience that have determined your appeal, not the needs of your congregation. Put down on paper in precise terms what you are offering.

3. *The Benefits of the Program or Service.* A list of the benefits that can be derived from the program you are offering will help you write strong, forceful direct-mail copy. If you are sending out an invitation to a program for singles, spell out the exact benefits the recipient can expect: friendship, fellowship, information on coping as a single parent, learning to rebuild a shattered self-image after divorce, and so on.

Now you can begin to write your letter.

A Letter-Writing Formula

Robert Stone, in his book *Successful Direct Mail Advertising and Selling,* presents a formula for writing direct-mail pieces. While recognizing that not all successful direct-mail letters are written to formula, Stone points out that more often than not, success in this medium results from following a tried and proven method, rather than from trying to be creative or original. Here is his formula. It might be wise to follow it in trying your hand at this type of letter-writing for the first time.

1. "Promise a benefit in your headline or first paragraph—*your most important benefit.*" Here Stone stresses the importance of putting your best foot forward to capture the prospect's attention immediately. The "lead" will either "hook" the prospect or let him swim nonchalantly away.

2. "Immediately enlarge upon your most important benefit." It is important to follow through on a good attention-catching headline, or you will lose the prospect's interest.

3. "Tell the reader *specifically* what he is going to get." The reader knows little or nothing about what you are offering. Give all the facts you possibly can. Try to anticipate in advance the kind of questions that might be asked. Tell the reader the benefits he or she can expect from a program.

4. "Back up your statements with *proof* and *endorsements.*" Don't be afraid to use testimonials from a third party. If they are simple and sincere, they will help build believability in your letter.

5. "Tell the reader what he might lose if he doesn't act."

6. "Rephrase your prominent benefits in your closing offer."

7. "Incite action—NOW!"

"This formula will never write copy for you, but it well may help you to include all the essentials to successful, resultful letters. It is worth a try."[2]

The postscript to a letter can also be very useful. Often a person will peruse a letter before reading it through. If so, there is a good likelihood that the first things he will read will be the signature and the postscript. Because the body of the letter will more than likely be a printed form letter, I suggest that the P.S. be personal and handwritten. This will increase readership and response.

Recently I received a letter that had no return address. However, it was postmarked Phoenix, Arizona, and that immediately aroused my curiosity. Also, my address was not mechanically reproduced, so I assumed the letter must be from an individual, or at least a small organization. Inside, all I found was an advertisement that had been torn out of a newspaper. The ad offered to show me how to "inflation-proof" my savings if I would purchase a new book which promised *The Ultimate Plan of Financial Self-Defense for the Small Saver and Investor.* I would just have tossed the ad aside if it had not been for a handwritten note along the margin: "Really worth reading! R." I did not have the faintest clue as to who R is, and I still don't, but his or her handwritten postscript almost persuaded me to spend $14.95 for that book. Only one thing stopped me. I didn't have any savings!

TEST! TEST! TEST!

In sending out a direct-mail letter, there is always the concern that we might have done a better job. Maybe another type of letter would have had a better response. With direct mail, this can be determined by testing. We can know, within certain limits, whether we have the best possible letter.

If your mailing consists of only 500 letters, then it would be impossible to run a test. However, just by way of example, let us suppose that your church is sponsoring a businessman's luncheon. Wishing to attract a minimum of 100 businessmen, you have decided on a mailing of 10,000 pieces. Rather than drafting one letter and mailing it out to all 10,000 names, it would be better to design three different letters—mail all of them on the same day, and to the same geographical region. Include in your mailing a response card to be returned, indicating that the individual will attend. Code the response cards A, B, or C, or print them on different colored paper, so that you can tell how many responses you receive from each letter. This test will determine which of the three was most effective.

Three Important Questions

1. *How long should a letter be?* There does not seem to be a firm answer to this question. Some direct-mail advertisers feel that one side of one page is the maximum length. They reason that when people receive an envelope that has been stuffed with a long letter, they will probably lay it aside until later, but you really want them to read it and act immediately. Or they may not want to take the time to read such an epistle and may never look at it again!

85

Other advertisers, however, have found through testing that a two-page letter ordinarily will outpull a one-page letter. Still others believe that "the more you tell, the more you sell." They feel that key to long copy is *facts*, just as in display ads. It is important to use small paragraphs and emphasize important points by underlining. Maybe this is one of the things you could test to find out which works best for you. One word of caution: Whether you use one page, two pages, or five, do not cram your copy in. Make sure that there is lots of white space, especially between paragraphs.

2. *How many pieces are there in an effective mailing piece?* Research indicates that the most effective mailing unit consists of an outside envelope (obviously!), a letter, a circular, a reply form, and a reply envelope, if necessary. Occasionally an additional piece will increase the response.

Whether you use a reply card (postcard) or a reply coupon and envelope, make sure that one or the other is included in your mailing. Make it easy for your prospect to respond. Leave lots of space for his name and return address on the card. State on the card what your prospect can expect from you.

Please send me my free copy of . . .
Enroll me in your Family Life Seminar . . .
I would appreciate knowing more about
Clayton Community Church . . .

3. *What size mailing should be sent?* For the most part, the answer to this question will be determined by the number of people you want to attract to a particular program or service. If you want to reach 15 people, it means you should send out 1,000 letters (response rate of 1.5 percent assumed). Your budget also helps determine the size of the mailing. While it is impossible to set an upper limit on the size of a mailing, we can set some minimums and draw some general conclusions.

One of the major problems that faces churches moving into advertising for the first time is that their initial attempts will be on the modest, or feeble, side. Several hundred letters will be sent out, with a large response expected. When there is no response, they give up. They fail to realize that a large-scale approach is required to achieve even a small success. Your church should send out a minimum of 500 letters per mailing, and if it wants to achieve any measure of success with direct mail, it should be sending out a minimum of 5,000 letters a year. However, do not let an arbitrary figure set the size of your mailing. Taking into account a reasonable response rate, let your objective determine the number of pieces you send through the mail.

A Strategy for Churches

The last quarter of the twentieth century is increasingly becoming the age of specialization, and while it is not yet widely recognized, this has become true of the Church today. Gone are the days of general programs meant for everyone. People are looking for specific programs or services to meet their own personal needs. Any church that wishes to be successful and effective in terms of ministry must recognize this fact.

The following strategy for identifying prospective new members is based on the principle of specialization and utilizes direct-mail evangelism.[3] The first step in this strategy is to identify a need in your community that is not being met by anyone else. Robert Schuller claims that "the secret of success is to find a need and fill it; find a hurt and heal it."

Now, there are two ways to identify the hurts and needs of your community. The first is speculation. The pastor and the evangelism committee get together and speculate about the needs they feel people have. This can be dangerous. Often our perception of reality and actual reality are two completely different things. You may be designing a program for a nonexistent need.

The other approach to need-identification requires more work, but it is safer in the long run. It is very simply to ask people—to survey your community. Peter Wagner once illustrated this point with the following true story.

> One pastor in a new area with an abundance of young families discovered, after deploying his lay people for a survey of the local populace, that the largest perceived need was for "potty training."

Realizing that the Bible called upon parents to "train up a child in the way that he should go" (Prov. 22:6), this pastor set up a one-day seminar on potty training, brought in an expert to speak on the subject, and then advertised it in the community. Not only did the seminar attract a significant number of young parents, but a number of these opened up their lives to God and began coming to the church.

The best way to identify a need is to ask—What is your greatest need right now?

Once you have identified a need, the second step is to design a program to meet that need. It may be a Christian day-care center, an exercise class for young housewives, a singles ministry to the recently divorced, or a morning Bible study for senior citizens, to name a few possibilities.

The third step is to design a letter, following the principles set down in this chapter, which will then be sent to everyone who can be identified as fitting into that category—parents with young children, young housewives, the recently divorced, or senior citizens. Ways to develop this list will be touched on later.

The response to your mailing will depend upon:

1. the accuracy of your survey and your perception of needs;
2. the design of the letter;
3. how well you have identified prospects;
4. the size of your mailing.

The final result of the program in terms of attracting people to your church will depend upon:

1. whether those who respond find that your program delivers what it promises;
2. how open and receptive your church members are to new people; and
3. whether there is a definite process set up to draw these new people into the life and fellowship of your church.

Sounds like a lot of work? You bet it is, but no one promised you that church growth and ministry are easy, or an automatic kind of thing. Lyle Schaller has compared making a church grow to pumping water uphill: When you stop pumping, it immediately runs back down the hill. If you are looking for something easy, be willing to accept decline. It's the path of least resistance.

Prospecting

The above strategies are based on the use of a mailing list. This may require renting a mailing list from a commercical concern that specializes in direct-mail advertising. Their mailing lists often are broken into thousands of categories and are useful to pinpoint prospects in a particular area.

If you desire to reach people in a certain geographical area, then a city directory or a post office directory that lists names and occupations would be helpful.

A third possibility is a list made up from a variety of directories, public records, and of course, word of mouth. New people who have moved into the area are some of the best prospects for a church. Some possible sources for the names of new people:

—Welcome Wagon or related agencies
—public utilities (gas, hydro [electric], water)
—real estate agencies (salespeople)
—corporation personnel managers
—moving companies
—church members living in the area.

One Final Tip

One excellent way to stimulate Sunday morning attendance is to develop a mailing list of your own. This list would be composed of the names of members (regular and otherwise), adherents (regular and not so regular), people from the surrounding area who have visited your church, parents of children in your church school, people who have come to you for counseling and weddings, and other similar prospects. Sending out regular mailings to these people will encourage and stimulate them to attend your services. Your mailing can inform them of a special service; it can tell them about a message or a series of messages you will be preaching—positive, hopeful, and helpful messages; or it could be simply a word of encouragement to let them know you care. Whatever the occasion, be sure to follow the ideas we have suggested for making sure your letters are opened and read.

VIII

Broadcast Advertising

With broadcast advertising, the first medium that comes to mind is television. However, in terms of cost, it is beyond the financial reach of the vast majority of congregations. It is in the big league, and if you have the capabilities to use this medium, you will need more in the way of expert advice than I am able to give you. So in this chapter, I will deal exclusively with radio advertising.

Radio has some pretty impressive things in its favor. Because it is flexible and can go wherever people go, radio reaches more people in a day than either television or newspapers. It reaches them at home, in the park, on the beach, at the office, and in 95 percent of all automobiles. Its reach, or "circulation," has grown much faster than that of either television or newspapers, and rates, on a percentage basis, have not increased as greatly. As one advertiser pointed out to me recently, radio can deliver more advertising impressions than any other medium, and for the same budget.

Switching from print to broadcasting will require some changes in our perspective. The major change is in terms of time. In the case of a newspaper ad or a direct-mail piece, serious prospects have the opportunity to scrutinize it several times until they have grasped the message, or at least picked up the pertinent points. I do not mean to suggest that this always happens with print ads, but it is a possibility.

No such opportunity exists with radio. You have ten, thirty, or at the most, sixty seconds to get your message across. If you have not made an impression by that time, or if the listener has not grasped your essential message, then you have lost your opportunity.

Another thing to consider is that it is rare for a person to just sit down and listen to the radio. People sit down and concentrate when they read a letter, scrutinize the paper, or watch television; but not radio. It is listened to while driving, while doing housework, or while at the office. Frequently it is just background noise to keep a person company. Half the time, the listener's attention is focused on something else. The trick is to gain the attention of an inattentive listener.

How Long Should It Be?

Commercials vary in length. Make sure you pick the length that is most economical, but still does the intended job. A radio commercial usually is referred to as a *spot*. Here are the standard commercial lengths:

1. *60-second spot*—ample time to present a complete message along with an identifying logo or theme. A 60-second spot is more expensive than a 30-second spot. It does not reach more people than a 30-second commercial—just the same people for a longer period of time. Go with a 30 if it will do the job;

2. *30-second spot*—delivers a message containing up to 75 words, long enough to be specific and short enough to be economical;

3. *20-second spot*—provides good support and serves as a reminder of information heard in longer commercials;

4. *15- and 10-second spots*—useful as memory joggers.

Use Radio's Selectivity to Target Your Market

One important characteristic of radio is its selectivity. It permits you to select your target market, or audience, with a fair amount of accuracy. Rarely do people listen to programs they do not like. Because of the multiplicity of stations, a listener can be very selective—choose either morning talk shows or the news; hard rock, classical, or country and western stations. If it is teenagers you want to reach, aim at a station that caters to their type of music and at a time when they will be home from school. But if homemakers are your target, morning talk shows or easy-listening music stations probably are a better bet.

Each station has its own distinct audience profile. Specific programs are built around listener preference, based on research. In selecting a station (if you have more than one to choose from), look for the one that reaches the kind of audience you feel would be interested in your church. Also note the size of the audience (the *reach*), so that you can compare rates.

The following kinds of information should be available from the BBM—Bureau of Broadcast Measurement (Canada) or from Arbitron (U.S.), which your local station will have and probably will let you examine. The following tables give figures for two fictitious radio stations, APOR and CDOG.

AGE CATEGORIES

Age Group	APOR Listeners	CDOG Listeners
3–11	3,700	4,000
12–17	10,900	5,500
18–24	12,200	3,100
25–34	19,900	19,800
35–49	17,900	18,500
50–59	15,700	12,100
60 & over	21,000	23,000
Total Weekly Audience	101,300	86,100

OCCUPATIONAL PROFILE

Occupation	APOR	CDOG
business owner/manager	4,200	4,600
professional	8,000	9,800
clerical	3,300	4,700
sales	2,200	1,800
farmer	500	1,900
skilled labor	8,900	7,800
unskilled labor	7,700	11,300
unclassified	59,900	38,500

Obviously, if farmers are your target market, then CDOG is the station to use, but if you want to reach young people from twelve to twenty-four years of age, then APOR should be your choice.

Can You Afford It?

Cost and the size of your church's advertising budget are definite considerations when considering whether radio is the medium you should use. The cost of a 30- or 60-second spot, depending on whether or not it is in prime time, may not necessarily be expensive; but to have that spot repeated with sufficient frequency for it to be grasped by your audience will probably run up quite a bill. Frequency is one of the keys to successful radio advertising. If you only have a minibudget to work with, steer clear of radio. It will not permit you to advertise often enough for your message to be heard. It will have a tendency to get lost in the air waves. You will get more mileage from your advertising dollar with newspapers or with direct mail.

To determine your cost for an effective radio advertising campaign, ask your local station for a rate card. Following is rate information for APOR, which will give you an idea of the way the rate structure for radio advertising works. These rates are for the purpose of illustration only. Costs will vary according to locality and also will be influenced by inflation.

BREAKFAST—5 A.M. to 9 A.M., Monday–Friday
    60-second spot $40
    30-second spot $26
MIDDAY—9 A.M. to 3 P.M., Monday–Friday
    60-second spot $45
    30-second spot $30
DRIVE-HOME—3 P.M. to 7 P.M., Monday–Friday
    60-second spot $14
    30-second spot $ 9
EVENINGS—7 P.M. to 12 P.M., Monday–Friday
    60-second spot $ 8
    30-second spot $ 8 (minimum rate)
WEEKENDS—6 A.M. to 8 P.M., Saturday & Sunday
    60-second spot $16
    30-second spot $11

The reasons for APOR's rate structure can be understood when we study the following statistics, which show the average audience by time block.

Monday–Friday	6 A.M.–10 A.M.	10,000
Monday–Friday	10 A.M.– 3 P.M.	6,200
Monday–Friday	3 P.M.– 7 P.M.	1,900
Monday–Friday	7 P.M.–12 P.M.	1,200
Saturday	7 A.M.– 7 P.M.	3,400
Sunday	7 A.M.– 6 P.M.	2,300

One way to increase your advertising frequency and reduce your cost is through the use of public-service announcements. It is possible that your local station will make these announcements at no charge, if you advertise to some degree. One or two public-service announcements a day will not give you effective radio advertising, but used in conjunction with a planned advertising program, they will lighten the financial load while maintaining or increasing frequency.

Radio time is bought most efficiently by taking advantage of packages and discount plans available to regular users. If your radio campaign is consistent and well planned, you probably will be able to buy the *end rate,* the lowest earned rate at which the station sells time.

From my perspective, radio probably would be most useful as a backup. Using this approach, newspaper would be your primary medium and would take up the bulk of your mass media advertising budget. Newspaper ads provide the continuity that is so necessary to a successful advertising effort. They can keep your message before the public on a continuous basis. Radio would be used to reinforce your message at peak times of the year—Christmas, Lent, Easter, and September. It would provide added frequency during those periods when people are most likely to go to church.

Designing Radio Advertising That Attracts

1. Aim at One Big Idea

Nothing is impossible, but trying to present more than one big idea on radio, with all the accompanying distractions, maybe is close to it. A cluttered commercial will blend in with the background noise. Emphasize only one idea or program—a well-designed church school; a community-wide program; a warm, caring fellowship; exciting, need-filling messages. Do not be caught in the trap of thinking you have to tell everything at once.

2. Use Distinctive Sounds to Gain Recognition

One of the best distinctive-sound commercials is "Ding dong, Avon calling!" which is familiar to millions. One hears the sound of the doorbell and almost automatically fills in the rest. Those commercials have helped make Avon a household word. Suggestions for distinctive sounds that you might use are: an easily recognized voice; warm, friendly conversation; church school children

99

laughing; a contemporary hymn tune. Steer clear of music like "Amazing Grace" or "Rock of Ages," unless you are pushing a Seniors Sing-Song. If you use music, keep it simple and do not use too much. You are trying to communicate a message, not entertain your audience.

3. Use Picturesque Language to Stir the Imagination

In a sense, radio is a visual medium of communication. Its uniqueness lies in the fact that it has power to stir the imagination. The advertiser who uses radio tries to create word pictures which can be viewed with the mind's eye. Oftentimes pictures created in this way are more powerful than visual effects created by film or television. To use radio advertising effectively, it is important to keep this in mind.

4. Speak Directly to the Prospect

Radio is also a very personal form of communication. Design your advertising so that it seems you are talking directly to the prospect, and make sure you write the ad the way people speak. Avoid stilted, convoluted language, and don't be afraid of contractions or colloquialisms.

5. Name Your Church and Its Benefits Early in the Commercial

This helps to create awareness. It also helps if the listener loses interest part way through the commercial. If you begin by saying who you are, then you will at least have kept your name before the public. If you wait until the end to identify yourself, and your listener has lost interest at mid-point, you have accomplished nothing. Actually, it doesn't hurt to mention who you are and what you can do for people several times during the commercial.

6. Watch Your Words

Keep them simple. The radio listener has no time to contemplate their meaning or to go back and think them over. Avoid confusing pronouns such as *we* and *our*. The listener may have trouble distinguishing to whom these refer, but there can be no mistaking the meaning of *you* and *your*. Finally, avoid tongue twisters and words that are hard to pronounce.

Remember, radio's unique strength is its ability to stretch and stimulate the listener's imagination. If you can use voices and various other sounds to create a mental picture, keeping in mind the other elements outlined above, then you will be well on your way to creating good, attractive, radio advertising.

IX

Some Alternative Places to Advertise

Newspaper, radio, and direct mail are the big three where you are most likely to spend your advertising dollar. But don't neglect other possibilities. Depending on your church and situation, one of the alternative mediums may prove to be more effective in reaching your target audience. Don't be afraid to use your imagination to come up with some exciting possibilities that I may not even have considered.

The Yellow Pages

I read recently that the phone book is a dull, static medium, with only minor advertising value. Don't believe it. It is true that, to date, the Yellow Pages have had only minor advertising value as far as churches are concerned. But that is because, apart form a phone number and address, churches do not advertise in the Yellow Pages. They take a free listing and let it go at that. At present, there is only one display ad in the Niagara Falls, Ontario, directory under "Churches," and that is for Chippawa Presbyterian Church. Check out your Yellow Pages and see how many churches in your area advertise there.

There are two facts you should know about Yellow-Page users. According to surveys, they are likely to be younger, rather than older adults. And most who use those pages follow up with a call, a visit, or a letter. A dull, static medium? No, I don't think so. People who use the Yellow Pages are looking for something. They are good prospects who are prepared to take action. If yours is the best, or maybe even the only display ad on the church page, there is a good chance that the prospect will call or visit your church.

Here are some tips that will help you design better Yellow-Page display ads.

1. *Let your ad perform a marketing function.* Don't just print the times of services and address. Stress those things your church does best:

   9:30—Informal Worship Service
   with Contemporary Music
   Solo—A Singles Program for Young Adults
   Weekday Nursery-School Program

2. If you are not located on a well-known street, *provide either a simple map or a one-line description of your location:*

   One Block South of City Hall
   Across from East Gate Plaza

3. *Use a drawing or photograph* to catch the

103

reader's attention. Try to make it people-centered, not just a shot of your church building.

4. *Stress the benefits your church can provide* for the person who is shopping for a church.
5. *Include the logo* of your congregation or denomination in the ad, and a distinctive slogan, if you have one.

The Church Sign—An Obvious Choice

There is nothing more frustrating when you are driving than to come upon a church with a small, postage-stamp-sized sign that is impossible to read. Many of them appear to have been designed during the days of the horse and buggy, not for the 1980s.

When designing a church sign, keep the following in mind.

1. A sign parallel to the road is fine for pedestrians and is probably more aesthetically pleasing, but it is impossible for car riders to read. *Put up a sign that is at right angles to the road* and which can be read from a car traveling at the speed limit in either direction.
2. *Make it big enough* to be read easily. On a street with a 60 kph (40 mph) speed limit, a 4 x 8 foot sign would be about right. Place it as close to the road as city ordinances permit.
3. *Aim at legibility.* That means using very plain and easily read block letters. Avoid fancy lettering and never, never, never use an "Olde English" script. It is difficult to read, and

besides, it gives the church an archaic air. That is not the kind of image you want to project.

4. *Keep your sign simple.* The most effective probably are those made of 4 x 8 foot sheets of plywood in a 4 x 4 inch cedar frame. It is doubtful that the sign made of brick or angelstone, surrounded by shrubs, and with a changeable print board enclosed in glass, is worth the expense.

5. Along with a listing of the times of worship and church school, *include a phrase or slogan* describing an essential characteristic of the congregation:

   Country-style Friendliness in the City
   A Warm Fellowship with People Like You

Billboards—Getting in the Big Picture

Some people find billboards objectionable, a blot on the landscape. If this characterizes your attitude on the subject, skip on to the next section. David Ogilvy of Ogilvy and Mather has denounced them as "bad advertising and worse citizenship." I will leave the aesthetic and ethical discussion to more erudite minds.

Whether you like billboards or not, the fact remains that increased awareness as a result of billboards can be impressive. And it appears that billboards are here with us to stay, so why not use the medium to communicate a really worthwhile message that could result in the fulfillment of a person's heartfelt need?

105

Outdoor advertising is a very unselective medium. It can cover a certain geographical area, but it cannot be aimed at a specific target audience. It must be aimed at a general audience, and that usually calls for a general message.

The cost of outdoor advertising varies from area to area. Billboards are usually rented on a *showing* basis. A *100 showing* indicates that an entire city, or geographical area, would be exposed to your advertising. A *25 showing* would cover the same geographical area but use only one-quarter as many billboards.

Billboards, in some instances, can be rented for a month, but usually a lengthy contract is involved. The cost is determined by the traffic location and the number of passersby, and is usually quite high.

All outdoor advertising resembles shooting at a moving target. You have only one fleeting moment—about 10 seconds—to communicate your message. You hold your readers longer only if they are caught in a traffic jam. Because of the time limitation, aim at communicating one single, solitary idea. If it is important in other advertising to have one big idea, it is even more important in outdoor advertising.

Here are some guidelines that will prove helpful in designing outdoor or billboard advertising.

1. *Brevity is the name of the game.* Restrict both the number of words and the pictures used—not more than six or seven words, and only one

picture. Remember, you have only ten seconds to communicate your big idea.

2. *Avoid fancy scripts and type.* Use bold, easily legible lettering that matches the bold message required in outdoor advertising. Your message must be readable from a distance, in a glance.

3. *Outdoor advertising is basically reminder advertising,* so use it in conjunction with other media. This is where a well-designed campaign approach pays off. Your billboard ad can reinforce an idea expressed in other media, but do not adopt billboards as a replacement for other well-conceived advertising.

And . . . And . . . And . . .

Actually, the possibilities of other places to advertise and other ways to advertise are limited only by your imagination and creativity. Here are just a few suggestions:

—signs on benches at bus stops and in other high-traffic locations

—transit advertising on buses and subways. If you consider building a clientele from transit riders, make sure the buses in your area run on Sunday.

—"holy hardware"—Have the name of your church printed on pens, pencils, and other items.

—T-shirts—These not only will advertise your

107

church, but build solidarity, as well as a sense of identity and belonging, among your members.

—a quarterly newspaper for mass distribution throughout your community.

Actually, the best advertising idea I ever had was one which ultimately failed. I was concerned with ways to reach new families moving into the community. Welcome Wagon had the contacts, but I knew they would not carry a brochure for an individual church, free of charge. So the only alternative was to pay them on the same basis as any other advertiser. I would then receive the additional benefit of the newcomer's name and address. There was only one hitch—Welcome Wagon's policy is not to accept religious or political organizations as clients. So it was back to the drawing board.

X

Setting an Advertising Budget

How much should you spend on advertising in a year? This is an important question, and over the years, both industry and the church have employed a variety of ways to arrive at an answer.

Let us examine the most common methods used to determine an advertising budget.

Affordable Method

Using this approach, in a particular year, a church spends as much on advertising as it thinks it can afford. If it is a good year financially, then money is made available for advertising. If it's a poor year, well . . . . This is one of the worst approaches your church can take. It fails to take into account the fact that a bad year may be the result of your failure to advertise. This type of approach shows a lack of planning, and in the end, the money usually is spent on something other than advertising.

Parity Method

Some churches set their advertising budgets on the basis of what other churches are spending. In industry, this is called *maintaining competitive parity*. A business will estimate its dollar sales for the next year and take a percentage of those sales as its advertising budget. The percentage figure is based on the average percentage commonly spent on advertising by the industry in which the firm is engaged. Here are sample figures for several types of businesses.

TYPE OF BUSINESS	AVERAGE ADVERTISING BUDGET (PERCENT OF SALES)
bookstores	1.5–1.6%
drugstores	1.0–3.0%
pet shops	2.0–5.0%
mail order firms	15.0–25.0%

Churches following this method would allocate .5 to 1.5 percent of their total budget for advertising.

The main argument for this approach is that it represents the collective wisdom of a church as to how much should be spent on promotion. My personal feeling, however, is that when it comes to advertising, that collective wisdom is rather suspect. A church using this method condemns itself to mediocrity in making its presence and program known in the community.

Percentage of Total Budget Method

This is the method Schuller suggested, and the one that started me thinking and planning seriously for advertising. Schuller maintained that a growing church should spend a minimum of 5 percent of its total budget on publicity. Declining churches should spend more.

This approach has much to recommend it. It is simple and easy to grasp. It represents a realistic figure and would appeal to those financially minded members of your congregation who feel that expenses of all types should bear a close relationship to your church's income. However, it has one major flaw, which is overcome by the next method.

Task Method

Using this approach, a church first must determine what it wants to achieve, and then determine the cost to achieve that objective. That cost then becomes the advertising budget for the coming year. In this approach, it is the *task*, and not what a church can afford, or an arbitrary percentage, that determines the budget. Rather than asking, What can we do with what we have? the task approach turns the question around and asks, What do we need in order to do what we should?

There are three stages to be followed in setting an advertising budget using this method:

1. define specific advertising objectives;
2. determine the tasks that must be performed in order to achieve these specific objectives;
3. estimate the cost of performing those tasks.

Two-hundred-fifty member Trinity Church was built in the mid-1960s on the growing edge of a small midwestern city. The church grew steadily during its first ten years, but since 1975, has hit a plateau. Noting the continued new development that is still going on only a mile away, and considering also the church's failure to reach out to the new families moving into the area, Trinity's leadership has made advertising a priority for the next few years. The question is, How much should they budget for advertising in the coming year? With an annual budget of $55,000, an arbitrary figure of 5 percent would involve an advertising budget of $2,750. Trinity's leadership, however, doubted whether $2,750 would do the job they wanted to do. To determine this, the communications committee worked through the various stages of the task method to arrive at a budget figure.

STEP 1: *Define specific advertising objectives.* The committee felt there were three specific things they wanted to accomplish through their advertising:

a. Create community awareness of Trinity Church as a progressive church with a people-centered ministry;

b. Attract 60 nonchurch people to Trinity's semiannual Family Life Seminars, as a means of introducing them to one ministry area of the church;

c. Attract new people to special services designed to acquaint visitors with the dynamic nature of Trinity's worship hour.

STEP 2: Determine the tasks that must be performed in order to achieve these specific objectives.

a. To create an awareness of Trinity Church, the committee felt that a series of ads 3 columns wide and 7 inches long, placed in a local weekly newspaper, would give them adequate coverage. This series would run 35 weeks out of the year and would coincide with those times of the year when people are most likely to attend church.

b. The committee felt a direct-mail campaign would be the best way to reach people for a one-time seminar. To attract 60 people, considering a response rate of 2 percent for first-class direct mail, would require a mailing of 3,000 letters.

c. For special services, the committee felt that a special 4-column by 10-inch newspaper ad should be run, along with six 30-second radio spots during the week preceding a service. Three special services were being arranged for the coming year.

STEP 3: Estimate the cost of performing those tasks.

Note: The following figures are for illustration only. Costs will vary according to locality and rate of inflation.

a. Newspaper Advertising
   3 columns @ $2.50 per column
   inch X 7 inches X 35 insertions $1,837.50

113

b. Direct-Mail Advertising
postage (first class)

3,000 letters @ 20¢	600.00	
paper @ $13.50 per 1,000	40.50	
envelopes @ $13.00 per 500	78.00	
	718.50	718.50

c. Newspaper

4 columns @ $2.50 per column inch X 10 inches X 3 insertions		300.00

d. Radio

3 30-second spots at breakfast time @ $26	76.00	
3 30-second spots at midday @ $30	90.00	
	166.00	
Repeat 3 times per year		496.00
Total Advertising Budget Using the Task Approach		$3,352.00

One factor you should consider in working out an advertising budget and media plan is the effect of inflation. One yardstick commonly used in the industry to measure the cost effectiveness of various media is the cost of reaching 1,000 people (CPM). A study done in 1977 shows the change in circulation and rates during a 5-year period in the early to mid-1970s.[1]

114

MEDIUM	PERCENT OF INCREASE		
	Rate	Circulation	CPM
daily newspapers	57.5	4.1	45.9
television—30-sec.	67.4	17.4	42.3
radio—30-sec.	45.1	29.9	11.8
outdoor	71.8	6.5	60.6

On a percentage increase basis, radio would appear, from these statistics, to be an increasingly cost-effective medium. With the lowest rate increase and the greatest circulation, or listenership, increase, the cost of reaching 1,000 people (CPM) rose less than 12 percent in 5 years.

One word of caution concerning the use of CPM is in order. In a campaign aimed at creating awareness of your church, it is a useful yardstick, but in terms of response, it can be a rather poor measuring device. For instance, radio may give you the greatest coverage for your dollar, but it also may give you a very low response rate for the specific programs or services you are advertising. Direct mail usually is the best route to follow if you are looking for a definite response rate.

XI

What If . . . It Works?

Once on the western prairies, there was a Canadian oil company that was faced with a disastrous oil well fire. For days it raged, defying all attempts to put it out. The company offered a large reward to anyone who could help. Experts were brought in from the Texas oil fields, but so intense was the heat that they could only come within 1,000 feet of the blaze, even with their asbestos suits. Finally, as a last resort, the company put in a call to the local volunteer fire department. An hour later, a battered red fire truck came bouncing across the prairie, and to the amazement of the assembled company officials, it rolled to a stop only 50 feet from the blaze. Out of the cab jumped a couple of good ole' boys who immediately hosed each other down and then proceeded to put out the fire. The company officials were impressed. Afterward, the president handed a large check to the chief of the volunteer brigade; and out of curiosity, he asked how the department would spend the money. "Well," the fireman replied, "the first thing we're gonna do is put new brakes on that blame truck!"

In a sense, that is what happened at Chippawa.

Advertising put us in a position where we had to do something, and fast. As the minister, I was forcibly struck by the fact that I had to have something to advertise. The old fare I had been dishing out every Sunday was in some ways monotonous and repetitious. That some change was in order quickly became apparent. I knew that a traditional Presbyterian worship service was meaningful to people who were raised with it, and a certain percentage of new people would expect that type of service and find their worship needs best met by it. But what about those who found a formal service a bit too much, who were looking for something a little more spontaneous and fresh and alive? I was especially concerned for those who had not been to church for a long time but now were beginning to come. How would they react? Would our services meet their deepest needs?

You see, traditionally, most churches have designed their worship services around one group of people—their members. It is not hard to understand why this happens. Most social organizations exist to serve the needs of those who belong to them. The problem is, however, that the Church does not exist just for itself. It has a strong missionary dimension. Just as its only King and Head was "the man for others," concerned "to seek and to save the lost" (Luke 19:10), so the Church as his Body exists for others as well. And those "others" are not members of other churches, but men and women who are completely outside the

Church—those who have not darkened a church door in five years, ten years, or maybe ever.

So I began to think about providing new worship opportunities that would meet a variety of needs. The first step was to provide options, and the easiest to provide was a time option. Rather than having only an 11:00 service and saying to people, Fit into what's convenient for us, we initiated another service at 9:30. This was more convenient for parents who had children in the church school or for people with noontime or early afternoon commitments. Then, too, there are people who just plain prefer the earlier hour. Most churches move to two services only after one service is filled and they are forced to make the change. That was not our position. We still had many vacant seats at 11:00 worship when we made the switch.

The second option we offered was in terms of the type of service. We kept the traditional worship service at the traditional 11:00 time for those who found that this approach best met their needs, but the 9:30 service was different. The atmosphere was more relaxed and informal. The music was more contemporary. We had a congregational sing-song built right into the service. One week, we would sing hymns and choruses that centered on a certain theme. The next, we had a "pick your own," which gave people an opportunity to exercise their musical preference. And we learned new pieces that were fresh and personal.

This whole approach was not intended in any way to neglect the constituent membership. It just

118

offered a greater choice to meet a wider range of needs.

After the church began to advertise and new people began to come, other glaring inadequacies made themselves apparent. We began to see that many of our traditions and procedures were designed for our members, people "in the know." Like a foreign language, these customs were unintelligible to outsiders and needed translation. Announcements in the Sunday bulletin referring to the Anna Gray (a women's group) and the W.M.S. (Women's Missionary Society) were intended for insiders. When it came to the Gloria Patria, the doxologies, and the choral amens in the traditional service, we just took it for granted that everyone knew them. Unfortunately, new people did not know them and stood there feeling rather foolish while everyone around them sang from memory.

Still another imperfection which came to light concerned greeters and ushers. We had never had greeters, and the ushers felt their duty was done when they handed out the bulletins. No one was helped to find a seat; brave and stalwart newcomers, especially if they were late, risked the long walk to the front alone. Our approach was fine for those who knew the ropes, but not for those who were new, particularly if they were unchurched.

We now had to ask ourselves questions we had never had to bother about before. Who were our programs designed for—our own members or unchurched people? The answer was very obvious. How did people see and perceive us? Was it as a

119

warm, friendly fellowship, or as a small, exclusive clique? Newcomers were excited about the church at first, but some soon left because of the lack of fellowship. Here was another area that needed attention.

The hardest question of all, though, had to do with our motives. Was our desire for numerical growth purely selfish? Was it a concern simply for the survival of an institution? Or were we concerned about meeting the authentic needs both of our members and of those who stood outside the saving, redeeming love of Jesus Christ? If we could not decisively answer that question, then our efforts were unworthy.

For Chippawa Presbyterian Church, it was the beginning of an adventure. We had a long way to go, and still have, but the path is now a little more clear. Advertising helped us make use of some of the principles that lead to church growth, in a way we had been unable to grasp before.

Now for some final considerations.

What Is Your Message?

What message are you trying to communicate? If we assume that, in broad outline, our target market is the unchurched, there are two considerations to keep in mind. The first is the need of the unchurched people in your community. If the message you communicate is not relevant to the needs those people have, then you are wasting your time and money. Second, keeping in mind people's needs, determine what you want your readers (or listeners) to think of your church. What kind of message do you want to project? Here are some possibilities:

—a dynamic, exciting church
—a friendly church with arms outstretched to lonely people
—a church with a message that is relevant and meaningful in our day
—a church filled with "your" kind of people— loving and accepting
—a church that provides encouragement and stimulation for daily living
—a servant church, concerned with meeting social and religious needs in the comunity
—a fun, active, and alive church that gives zest to life.

These are just possibilities. Do not let them limit you in any way. Only you can know what the people in your community need and what your church has to offer them. You are a unique institution in a unique situation.

Paying the Price

Church advertising does cost. And when I say that, I am not referring simply to that portion of your budget which covers promotion. The costs I am talking about are hidden; they never show up on a financial statement or in the annual report. It is the

121

cost of time expended in creative thought and strategy planning; the hours seemingly wasted when the church's governing body or the communications committee rejects a campaign you felt would have a tremendous appeal to the unchurched.

But above all else, church advertising is costly because there will be some members of your congregation who do not think it is a necessity and will oppose it. There will be one or two who feel that it is degrading to the church and to the denomination. "That's all right for those other denominations, but for our church, well . . ." Then there will be those who think that "our church has survived this long without advertising; why do we need to start that stuff now?" And sadly, there will be those who do not want the church to grow. It has provided them with a familiar, safe, and non-threatening environment over the years. They know everyone, and growth will mean that the "family" circle will be broken. These are some of the reasons people will resist an advertising program for your church.

Are you prepared to pay the price? An advertising campaign does not run just for a few months, but for years. You will be dealing with an approach that should continue on a consistent basis forever—or at least as long as a church exists. In other words, you are embarking on a costly, long-term endeavor. But remember, it is an endeavor that holds tremendous capability for influencing the religious attitudes and church-going habits of many within your community. The cost is a small price to pay for that glorious adventure in which we are involved—becoming all things to all men in order that we "might by all means save some" (I Cor. 9:22).

Notes

I. "In the Beginning . . ."

1. (Glendale, Cal.: G/L Publications, Regal Books, 1975), p. 146.

II. Why Advertise?

1. Philip Kotler, *Marketing Management: Analysis Planning and Control* (Englewood Cliffs, N.J.: Prentice-Hall, 1976), p. 341. Chart adapted from the Marketing Science Institute Series, *Personal Selling in a Modern Perspective*, by Patrick J. Robinson and Bent Stidsen. Copyright © 1967 by Allyn and Bacon, Inc., Boston. Used with permission.

IV. Advertising Strategy

1. This is known as the homogeneous unit principle of church growth. The key book in this area is C. Peter Wagner's *Our Kind of People* (Atlanta: John Knox Press, 1979).
2. From *Film Workshop Workbook and Planning Session Guide* (Garden Grove, Cal.: Robert H. Schuller Institute for Successful Church Leadership, 1980), p. 62. Used by permission of The Gallup Poll.

VII. Direct Mail

1. (New York: Ballantine Books, 1971), p. 80.
2. From pp. 98-101 in the book *Successful Direct Mail Advertising*

and Selling by Robert Stone, © 1955 by Prentice-Hall Inc. Published by Prentice-Hall, Englewood Cliffs, N.J. 07632. Used by permission.
3. The major work to date on direct-mail evangelism is Jimmie L. Gentle and Dale Alan Dauten's book, *Programmed Guide to Increasing Church Attendance* (Lima, Ohio: C.S.S. Publishing Co., 1980).

X. Advertising Budget

1. John Tomlinson, "National Media Costs to Increase by 11.8%," *Marketing* (January 17, 1977): 34.

126

CREATIVE LEADERSHIP SERIES
Edited by Lyle E. Schaller

Books to provide practical help in developing and administering a more effective church program, for both lay and clergy leaders.

—*Assimilating New Members* by Lyle E. Schaller
    01938-9
—*Beginning a New Pastorate* by Robert G. Kemper
    02750-0
—*Building an Effective Youth Ministry* by Glenn E. Ludwig
    03992-4
—*The Care and Feeding of Volunteers* by Douglas W. Johnson
    04669-6
—*Church Advertising* by Steve Dunkin
    08140-8
—*Church Growth* by Donald McGavran and George Hunter
    08160-2
—*Creative Stewardship* by Richard B. Cunningham
    09844-0
—*Leading Churches Through Change* by Douglas Alan Walrath
    21270-7
—*The Pastor's Wife Today* by Donna Sinclair
    30269-2
—*Preaching and Worship in the Small Church* by William H. Willimon and Robert L. Wilson
    33820-4
—*The Small Town Church* by Peter J. Surrey
    38720-5
—*Strengthening the Adult Sunday School Class* by Dick Murray
    39989-0
—*Time Management* by Speed B. Leas
    42120-9
—*Your Church Can Be Healthy* by C. Peter Wagner
    46870-1

$4.95, paper/each book (All prices subject to change.)

MAIL ENTIRE PAGE TO:

Customer Service Manager * Abingdon * 201 Eighth Avenue, South * Nashville, TN 37202
Send books checked to

Name _____
    (Please print or type)
Address _____

City _____ State _____ Zip _____

I am enclosing $_____(plus 65¢ to cover postage and handling).
*Please send check or money order—no cash or C.O.D. accepted. Please allow three weeks for delivery.